THE BGA GUIDE TO BUSINESS SCHOOLS

The BGA Guide to Business Schools

For Prospective Students
and Employers

Compiled by

Professor Tony Kennerley

Published for
THE BUSINESS GRADUATES ASSOCIATION LTD
28 Margaret Street, London W1N 7LB
Tel: (01) 637 7611/2

SIXTH EDITION

MACDONALD AND EVANS

Macdonald & Evans Ltd
Estover, Plymouth PL6 7PZ

First published 1970
Second edition 1973
Third edition 1976
Fourth edition 1979
Fifth edition 1981
Sixth edition 1985

© Macdonald & Evans Ltd 1985

British Library Cataloguing in Publication Data

Kennerley, Tony
    The BGA guide to business schools: for
    prospective students and employers. – 6th ed.
    1. Business education – Directories
    I. Title   II. Coulson-Thomas, Colin. BGA guide
    to business schools   III. Business Graduates
    Association
    658′.007′11   HF1106

    ISBN 0–7121–0663–4
    ISBN 0–7121–0659–6 (Pbk)

Photoset in Baskerville by
Northern Phototypesetting Co., Bolton
Printed in Great Britain by
Richard Clay (The Chaucer Press) Ltd,
Bungay, Suffolk

Foreword

The challenges of the 1980s will give the leaders of industry and commerce an opportunity to demonstrate every quality demanded of the modern manager. World recession, the grave structural problems of parts of British industry, and the need to transform technological advances into economic success will call for hard work, commercial ability and foresight on the part of British managers to a perhaps unprecedented extent.

Courage and resilience will be indispensable ingredients of successful management under these conditions. I am sure that British managers do have the ingredients for success; and the measures the Government has taken during its six years in office have at last begun to give managers the opportunity to manage and to reap the benefits from doing so successfully. The opportunities for management development described in this book will give to enterprising individuals a real chance to meet the challenge of the 1980s in ways which will benefit them and the society we all live in.

I am also conscious of the valuable work which business graduates are doing on a voluntary basis. BGA studies, for example, on professional management training in local Government and hospital administration, and on business studies in schools, have been useful additions to the information available to Government Departments. I appreciate too the Association's proposals on de-mergers, and look forward to a continuing close relationship between this Department and the BGA.

v

FOREWORD

I therefore welcome this latest edition of the Guide to Business Schools by the Business Graduates Association, and am confident that those who benefit from it will find ample opportunities to play a leading role in both the public and private sectors of our economy in transforming the challenges of the 1980s into real achievements.

Sir Keith Joseph
Secretary of State for Education and Science

Preface

This book is intended for prospective business school students and for personnel, recruitment, and management development managers.

At the time the Business Graduates Association was founded in 1967 very little information about business schools was available in Britain. The BGA therefore undertook as one of its first tasks the assembly and publication of factual and objective information about business schools at home and abroad, for the benefit of prospective students and employers. The result was a series of pamphlets, later consolidated into *The BGA Guide to Business Schools*. The first edition was published in 1970 and subsequent editions appeared in 1973, 1976, 1979 and 1981. The current edition, as well as being brought up to date, has been expanded and largely takes account of the changes over the past decade in the philosophy of business education and in the business school courses which reflect these changes. The book now covers over sixty schools world-wide. It is still the only such reference book in existence.

The BGA asked its Director, Professor Tony Kennerley, to compile this edition. The second, third and fourth editions were edited by Roger Frost, assisted by Andrew Lock, the successors to Kerin Lloyd and John Egan who produced the first edition. The fifth edition was compiled by Colin Coulson-Thomas. The Association is grateful to them all. We should also like to thank all those business schools and the many business graduates who have completed questionnaires and assisted in other ways in the production of the various editions of the Guide.

Every effort has been made to ensure the accuracy of the information in the book, but neither the Business Graduates Association nor the Editor nor the Publishers can accept responsibility for the accuracy of the information given.

Stephen Peach (Chairman)

1985

vii

Contents

CONTENTS

CHAPTER 1

Education for Business

INTRODUCTION

This book is about postgraduate management education and the
Graduate Business Schools which provide it.

The benefits to the individual of successfully completing a postgraduate course leading to a Master's degree in business are such
that the advice to any suitable person considering such a course
must be "If you get the opportunity to go to business school, grab
it!" Such a course is one of the most stimulating, demanding and
rewarding educational experiences available. The benefit is also
reaped by the employer of the business graduate through his high
motivation and his understanding and application of advanced management processes and techniques.

Outside the United States, however, there have been, until
recently, few business graduates on whom to test such statements.
For, measured on the timescale of the development of the classic
academic disciplines, the study of the management process is very
new. In Britain before 1960, for example, a discussion on what kind
of education would most suit a person for a career in industry or
commerce would probably have concentrated on two alternatives.
For those wishing to be at the "making" end of the business, engineering would have been suggested; while the classics (history,
economics, politics, etc.) would have been recommended for those
wishing to go into administration.

The idea of a formal educational programme specifically for and
about business was regarded with suspicion, and, except for one or
two exceptions (e.g. University of Aston and University of Manchester Institute of Science and Technology), was largely ignored by
academia and industry in the United Kingdom.

The change that took place in Britain in the late 1960s and early
1970s was remarkable. These years saw the creation of the University Business Schools, providing in most instances postgraduate

1

study in business and management (though a few also have under-graduate programmes); and the development, through the Council of National Academic Awards, of numerous undergraduate pro-grammes in business studies mainly in polytechnics with some of these now offering postgraduate work. Doctoral programmes have also emerged to train teachers for the new business schools.

Such rapid change – and in terms of education development, the growth of formal business and management education in the UK is very rapid – has inevitably given rise to controversy and debate, and, although most of the heat has dissipated, the debate still proceeds on many issues. One of them is the educational versus training role of formal business education. It is naturally of concern that in college-based courses leading to formal degree qualifications academic rig-our be incontestable. At the same time, however, the subject content must be relevant to business and to the pursuit of a career in busi-ness. Furthermore, some areas of study in business education are so new in academic terms that the existence of a valid "body of know-ledge" which can be imparted has only recently been accepted by the more traditional academics. The leading business schools are now playing an important role in the development of the manage-ment disciplines.

THE STRUCTURE AND AIMS OF BUSINESS SCHOOL COURSES

Graduate Schools of Business or Management now rest more easily within the University structure, the traditional home of learning, and most industrialists no longer see the development of academic rigour as unsuitable for business education. Businessmen are con-cerned that business education should deal with practical reality, not with academic excellence, and the schools have been at pains to ensure that courses meet this demand. The academic community's value and career system of research, theorising and publication, however, is still regarded by many in the so-called real world as difficult to relate to the problems of profitability, industrial relations and the other pressing matters of the day.

Businessmen's fears are no longer well founded, if indeed they ever were. And it is the academic approach which made them uneasy that has produced the body of knowledge, now admitted to exist within business schools, relating to the management of people and resources. More and more throughout the world, acceptance is growing that this knowledge can be used to advantage over a wide range of operations. At the same time, more and more companies are co-operating closely with the major business schools for research and analysis into specific problems to which only an academic

2

approach can do full justice. It is this co-operation which enables the body of knowledge to grow, and for techniques and processes of practical value to be developed from it.

The need for advanced techniques has become steadily more evident in recent years. The increasing rate of technological change, and the dramatic increase in the size of industrial units, have meant that managers are required to make more, and increasingly complex, decisions which require relatively precise information and analysis. Coupled with this there has been, since the war, a considerable levelling of hierarchies based on position alone and an increasing questioning of management and authority in general. Meritocracy had advanced.

The sanctions available to management have been eroded over this period because arbitrary sanctions are no longer acceptable in our society. This has been compounded by the increasing distance between the manager and those affected by his decisions. Recently more emphasis has been placed upon the benefits of de-mergers. Management authority now stems principally from the degree to which the individual manager's judgment is trusted and the level of respect in which he is held. The relationship between formal business education and management practice is relevant to this, business education being seen as one way in which the decision making process can be improved. It used to be widely held that no one can be taught to become a good manager, and until recently business schools would have said that they were not trying to develop managers, but to teach skills to help people become better managers. Now some may be shifting their stance, as effective management tends to depend as much on teachable skills as on personal qualities.

Some people differentiate between the study of business and the study of management. Others see "business studies" as but another phrase for "management studies". Government departments draw a distinction, however, so that in many British colleges there are two separate departments – one for business studies and one for management studies. The basis for the distinction lies in the hypothesis that the nature of courses and instruction for those young persons without business experience, but aspiring to careers in business, is necessarily different from courses and instruction most beneficial to those older persons who have some business experience, and who are undergoing further training, education and development. This question of differentiation is as yet unresolved. Some argue that business cannot be taught but that management techniques can.

What are the results to be sought and expected from formal college based courses in business and management? Given that learning by experience, which was virtually the only means hitherto available, is too slow and too uncertain for the latter half of the twentieth century, the desired result of business education must be that of accelerated learning on the one hand, and concurrent understanding on how to apply what has been learned on the other. To achieve this result for people with differing needs, three separate education processes have evolved: one designed for people without experience of business but who wish to make their careers in it; another designed for those already in industry who wish to increase their capabilities in their present roles, and by so doing improve their potential for other roles; and a third process recognised as attempting to analyse phenomena found in business, and to develop the theories which can explain, predict and offer means of controlling various situations.

Not all courses fall clearly into one of these categories. An example of one that does is the Sloan programme, designed for middle management people of top management potential, and offered by the London Business School, and by Stanford and MIT, where it originated. Another is the Diploma in Management Studies, a course for practising managers, limited to people over twenty-three years of age with a minimum of two years of business experience, and holding either a degree or a professional qualification. It is run at about forty colleges in Britain, each teaching its own particular programme within a common curriculum. The Council for National Academic Awards monitors programmes and awards the Diploma to successful students.

First degree and higher degree courses in the United Kingdom and elsewhere do not fit so neatly into the outline classification. They have varied objectives, although Bachelor courses are essentially preparatory, while Masters courses are mainly post-experience. Only a small minority of students on first degree courses have business experience whilst on Masters courses, more especially in the UK, the proportion of students with business experience ranges from 60 per cent to 100 per cent. In the United States the proportion tends to be lower.

Most generalist Masters programmes in business studies do not stipulate a first degree in business as a prerequisite, and so differ from most other Masters programmes which are a continuation of first degree study. All postgraduate programmes in business studies accept a wide range of professional qualifications and first degrees, though preference is sometimes shown towards numerate first degrees, and numeracy is stressed in most Masters programmes.

With such a wide net, study necessarily starts at basics, and minimal knowledge in the curriculum study areas is usually assumed. Thus the starting point for many Masters programmes is also the starting point for many first degrees in business; once the basics have been covered, the courses diverge, and thereafter the level of study, the depth to which subjects are explored and the speed by which progress is made then differentiate the undergraduate and graduate programmes. First degrees cannot, and should not, go into intellectual depth of study areas that good Masters programmes must go. Few of the major British University Business Schools have developed undergraduate programmes, as most believe that business being complex, dynamic and multi-disciplinary is more effectively studied at the postgraduate level. There has however been considerable growth in Britain in sandwich and part-time courses at Polytechnics, leading to business studies degrees awarded by the CNAA. Some of these courses are spread over a number of years, with periods of industrial experience alternating with periods of study.

This pattern of an integrated study and work experience in the first degree programme is in contrast with the North American pattern which is much more module oriented. Students tend to be offered a choice of fairly self-contained modules each lasting a term (or quarter of semester, depending on the system used), and a combination of modules satisfactorily completed will lead to the award of the degree. Some modules are compulsory and some form a linked chain, the study of one being a requisite for the study of another. This system has the advantage of flexibility, easing the problem of continuous development but making integration of subjects difficult.

Masters programmes follow a similar pattern with the emphasis differing from school to school. Most of them stress quantitative analysis, behavioural aspects and policy issues, and some base the programme on general systems theory. Specialisations are common, ranging from functional (marketing, production, finance, personnel, etc.) to organisation (e.g. public administration, hospitals, etc.). In North America some business schools have developed separate programmes for persons interested in "non-profit organisations" and so a variety of courses, such as Masters in Hospital Administration, or Public Administration and the like, have developed over the years. Some schools also have close contacts with the military establishment and so look at military administrative problems. Joint programmes (e.g. law and business lead to JD/MBA degrees) are offered at a number of US schools.

These developments have caused problems of identity for certain Graduate Schools of Business who find themselves operating some very un-business courses, to which other departments may lay claim. Some schools have sought to resolve the problem by changing their name to Graduate School of Management. Doctoral programmes, designed primarily but by no means exclusively for people who intend to teach, are available at most business schools. There is, however, a continuing shortage of qualified candidates in this important field.

5

Education for business, in its many forms, is in essence one branch of the study of the management of people and resources grouped together for a variety of purposes. This explains the wide variety of courses specialising to a greater or lesser degree in business, public administration, hospital administration and other fields. Perhaps the way in which a subject is taught is more important than what is taught. Business schools aim both to train their students to cope with change and stress and a heavy and varied workload, and to develop a systematic approach to problem solving and the ability to work with a variety of personalities in group situations. The form and level of business education that an individual chooses must be very much a reflection of his assessment of his own needs, capabilities, aspirations and opportunities. It is therefore unsafe to make categoric statements as to the "best" form of business education; this book is designed to assist the reader to make a sound individual choice, and to assist companies in formulating policy for their own management development.

CHAPTER 2

Graduate Schools
of Business

THE PURPOSE AND GROWTH OF BUSINESS SCHOOLS

It is the problems of modern management methods that the Graduate Business Schools direct their attention, to develop and teach theory, processes and techniques and their practical application to those who aspire to make their career in management.

The debate on the utility and practicality of business schools is long over in the United States, where business education can effectively be said to have started with the foundation of the Wharton School at the University of Pennsylvania in 1881. However, the concept of the postgraduate degree in business can more accurately be said to have originated with the foundation of the Harvard Business School in 1908, based on the very successful model of the Harvard Law School. Now there are over 300 postgraduate business schools in the USA with an annual graduate output of some 60,000.

In the United Kingdom (while there are exceptions such as the University of Manchester Institute of Science and Technology Department of Administration which was founded in 1918, Henley which offered its first course in 1948, and a business seminar at the LSE), the growth of business education dates from the publication of the Robbins Report in 1963, recommending the creation of high quality business schools in, or as adjuncts to, universities. The creation of the Foundation for Management Education in 1960 also contributed to the new awareness of the need for top-level business education as well as the more vocational training traditionally the province of the technical college. The Franks Report, a detailed study of the implementation of the Robbins recommendation, resulted in the foundation of the London and Manchester Business Schools as centres of excellence sponsored jointly by industry and the University Grants Committee.

Since then, expansion has been quite rapid and in the UK there are now over forty schools and universities offering postgraduate courses in business studies, representing an output of some 1,200 graduates per annum. There are, in addition, a substantial number of other institutions offering courses relevant to business. The quality and nature of business schools, however, vary greatly. Not all UK schools feature on the "list" of the Business Graduates Association (BGA).

In continental Europe, there are relatively few graduate business schools of a type that would be recognised as such in the US and the UK. The most renowned are mainly financed through industrial trusts and do not have close ties with traditional universities. Business "Grandes Écoles" are emerging in France, while in Germany an engineering training tends to provide the "route in" for the intending business high-flyer.

However, the lack of the typical business school in Europe should not be mistaken for a lack of interest in the development of business and management education. Different educational systems have found different answers to the study of the management process. In some countries, management education is thoroughly and effectively integrated into technical courses; in others, traditional institutions have adapted to meet the need, and have largely gone unnoticed in the international scene, lacking the glamour of the big league business school. During the last decade, an acceleration in the growth of business schools worldwide could be detected. Australia, Brazil, Israel, Japan, South Africa and Spain (and formerly Iran) all now have major institutions which are recognised internationally and this trend is reflected in the BGA "list" of schools and this *Guide*.

In Britain, as in America, the close relationship between business schools and the universities has led to the development of the concept of the intellectual challenge of management and the opportunity for putting ideas into practice. They have sufficient independence from industry to be able to ensure that the individual is not merely trained for a function but acquires a more general education as a form of personal development. Some tension between employers and business schools is inevitable and even desirable if the latter are to carry out their functions properly. Industry's needs, for example, are relatively short-term, as manpower planning finds it difficult to project beyond five years, yet the individual is being trained for a career spanning thirty or forty years in which many specialist skills will become outmoded. Therefore, while business schools need to communicate skills which are of immediate relevance on the job, they have also to provide education which will enable their graduates to adapt in a changing world. Today's theory may also be tomorrow's practice, and while business graduates may feel that too few companies at present use the advanced skills frequently taught at a business school, it would be foolish to ignore their future potential.

Business schools aim to develop the ability to analyse real-life situations while teaching the core discipline-based subjects, drawing on all these disciplines in an integrated fashion. The schools also teach students to be aware of social, political, economic and ethical considerations in reaching decisions and implementing them.

The basic disciplines which in one form or another are the foundation for many postgraduate business degrees are industrial relations and social psychology, mathematics and operations research, finance and accountancy, law, marketing, economics, production and business policy.

TEACHING TECHNIQUES AND BENEFITS

The approach to teaching varies from the discipline based approach, exemplified by Chicago, to the case study approach where all learning is set in practical situations, as in the Harvard archetypes; the majority of leading schools use a mixture of the two. Structures vary from the tightly programmed modular course to the more informal project-based type. In view of the wide differences between individuals in their learning capabilities, none of the various approaches can be said to be the most effective either singly, in combination, or in permutations.

Within the context of the content and the teaching approach, courses are then designed to teach students:

(a) how to work under pressure. All the good schools try to impose a high workload, so that students develop a capacity to produce reasoned reports quickly, to deal with many different subjects at the same time, and to perform effectively in competition with others;

(b) how the various core techniques are integrated and how the parts of an organisation react on one another to influence analysis and decision-making;

(c) a sound methodology of problem-solving, by recognition of key elements, identification of alternative actions, and selection of preferred action;

(d) how to work with other people.

Much of the benefit from a business school course comes from the exposure of the student to a concentrated group of highly intelligent people from backgrounds which may vary widely from his own. Taken together with the variety of ages and levels of experience, this leads to a constant dialogue between those committed to an idealistic viewpoint of social and economic change and those who have a committment to existing structures. Primarily, however, the result is a continuing intellectual stimulus, forcing the individual to present

9

arguments cogently and concisely and to subject these to criticism by his fellows.

At the end of it all, the student has to convince an employer of his worth. The letters after his name are only of interest to the employer in so far as they represent a selection process and a certain intellectual capacity. Essentially, the graduate must rely on his own abilities in dealing with employers and colleagues. Many of the latter will no doubt be suspicious of the new, probably younger, member of the team, and will need convincing about his personal qualities.

DEGREES AND LENGTH OF COURSE

The classic degree awarded by the business schools is the Master of Business Administration (henchforth referred to as MBA) though some schools award a Master of Science degree (MSc in the United Kingdom, MS or SM in the United States) for courses that are virtually identical, e.g. Massachusetts Institute of Technology and the London Business School. Those accepted for these courses normally have a degree or an equivalent professional qualification, though sometimes exceptions are made in the case of experienced managers with demonstrable intellectual ability.

The standard American MBA takes two years, though there are accelerated programmes in which exemptions are granted that permit the reduction of the course length. Only two major schools in the United Kingdom have followed the two-year model; the majority of the courses listed cover an academic or a calendar year. A number of schools now offer part-time evening MBA programmes. Certain institutions such as Cranfield and the London School of Economics have arrangements whereby students can take a second year in a United States school, and some operate exchange arrangements with the USA, South America and Europe during the latter part of the course. The continental schools are based on either one-year or nine-month courses. There is no optimum length for a business course as it depends on the individual and on age and experience; some prefer to spend as little time away from the work environment as possible, others take what they see as a rare opportunity to explore areas of interest and go for a two-year course.

Many believe there is no substitute for the intensive full-time MBA programme at a business school. These attract the staff, the industrial support, research, consultancy, curricula and knowledge. Management education is very much a participative, discussive and group activity and the business schools have an unrivalled capacity to provide the environment appropriate for maximum benefit to students.

And so what of the future? In the United States some over-all equilibrium seems to have been reached with general acceptance of the MBA and continual development of approaches to teaching. In Europe and the UK in particular, the explosive growth phase of full-time courses over the last decade has now ended, and it seems unlikely that many more will be established. Elsewhere, growth continues but at a more modest pace although it can be fairly confidently predicted that there will be growth in part-time courses in many countries. In America it is variously estimated that of the approximately 60,000 students enrolled on MBA type courses, two-thirds are pursuing part-time study at evening school, and the Business Schools in Britain are paying increasing attention to this form of study with a small number of part-time courses now available. Everywhere the emphasis is on practicality and relevance. Part-time Masters programmes will go some way towards satisfying the oft-stated need of industry to futher educate existing managers on the job.

of the 60,000 MBAs in US
2/3 are P/T. in evening

CHAPTER 3

The Employment of Business Graduates

OPPORTUNITIES AND PROSPECTS

The MBA qualification cannot be said to be a meal-ticket nor a guarantee of a high salary or a prestigious job in the long-term although there is strong evidence to suggest that for the new graduate the qualification is indeed such a meal-ticket, an entry to jobs carrying salaries higher than would be commanded normally by persons of the graduate's age and experience. However, it must be stressed that the ticket is only valid for at most a year or so. The ticket-holder must show himself (the masculine pronoun is used purely for the sake of simplicity) worthy of whatever post and salary he has used the ticket to help obtain for himself. If he cannot do this then the ticket *per se* is invalid. Put another way, the qualification is an indication of potential which, if not realised, disqualifies the holder, not the qualification. It does not matter how many qualifications a man possesses; if he cannot deliver the goods, he must go.

With these reservations, the prospects for a new business graduate with his MBA or MSc, are good. His skills are most needed in the dynamic situations of growth and technological or social change. He should not expect instant responsibility, but there are wide opportunities for promotion for those who can demonstrate their skills in the workplace. Future prospects, the nature of the task and the social environment are much more important than the starting salary after business school, and indeed many find one of the most useful aspects of business school is being able subsequently to be rather more selective in their choice of job, aiming for something with some intrinsic satisfaction.

It is certainly true that those with prior employment experience are much more marketable at the conclusion of the course than those who come straight from university. This is because:

(a) they are already adapted to the employment situation;
(b) being older they can fit more easily into a salary structure;

(c) they tend to be more useful in the short term;

(d) business experience probably helps students gain more from the formal programme.

Those with some knowledge of the world find it much easier to relate the business course to their own experience and thus gain substantially more from it. As with undergraduate courses, a little more maturity leads to greater benefits from contributions to the course. It is not always easy, though, owing to personal and financial commitments, to take one or two years off for a postgraduate course, thereby interrupting one's career. Immediate graduates find as a rule the basic disciplines easier than their fellows and are more in the habit of study, and can often, therefore, raise the intellectual pace of the course. Furthermore, after a business school course they have a marked advantage over the graduate who has not been to business school, and so, while the ideal scenario is to go to business school after a few years' business experience, going end-on to a first degree is much better than not going at all. This assumes in both cases the individual is capable of utilising the knowledge gained for his career.

From the firm's point of view, why recruit the new business graduate if after a year or so it is the track record that really counts? The following characteristics are common to the majority of business graduates.

(a) The business graduate is trained to take an over-all view of the organisation, its operations, objectives and strategy.

(b) He understands and has a reasonable degree of competence in a wide variety of business skills and functions, and can deal with problems of a high level of complexity, especially those that cut across the common functional divisions of business.

(c) He is of considerable intellectual ability, and is capable both of generating new ideas and of subjecting them to rigorous criticism and testing.

(d) Business school education, while committed to systems concepts and views, is also most appropriate to changing situations where new ideas and approaches are both needed and welcome.

(e) The business graduate has a considerable level of motivation and expects promotion (or demotion) in a company to be based on past achievements and future potential.

(f) The business school graduate is used to a high work load and considerable intellectual and mental pressure: he produces his best in challenging situations.

(g) Like other professionals, his relationship with the organisation is less one of blind commitment and dependence than a cool assessment of the mutual value of the relationship to himself and the employer.

In the light of these characteristics a series of ground rules can be established for the recruitment of a business graduate.

(a) There should be a positive and well-defined job specification. In other words, the employer should have evaluated an apparent need in his organisation and defined the type of skills required to carry out the function. These skills may then be compared with those possessed by a business graduate.

(b) The skills defined should be those necessary to carry out the function. Employing someone who is either under- or over-qualified for a position leads to dissatisfaction on both sides. The position offered to the business graduate should be one in which he is stretched to a reasonable degree and one in which his responsibility increases at a similar rate to his personal development. A business graduate without prior managerial experience should normally be employed in a staff function with some supervision, and should gradually be given line responsibility as he develops. It is just as much a mistake to give too much responsibility too fast as too little too slowly. However, as the business graduate may be expected to learn rapidly this process is usually accelerated well beyond the norm.

(c) There should be a well thought out promotion policy. The employers should be able to present career patterns that are possible given a reasonable degree of success. He should have considered the future opportunities that he can offer. The business graduate needs to be able to see approximately where he is going in order to sustain his motivation in a particular position.

These are of course no different in essence from rules to be followed in all managerial recruitment. They lead us naturally to a discussion of the pitfalls of employing a business graduate.

(a) The employer should avoid raising expectations above those that can be legitimately and reasonably fulfilled. It is quite easy to over-market a post, and one may therefore recruit someone over-qualified.

(b) The recruiter should consider whether the individual skills or temperament of a particular business graduate make him suitable for a specific post.

(c) Some companies have attempted to find employment for business graduates "to see what they can do". Often a real job has been lacking, which has led to mutual disillusion.

(d) It is quite often easy when "selling" a job to find examples of previous recruits who have risen to great things. However, care should be taken to avoid the use of unusual exceptions as examples.

(e) In fairly static employment situations, difficulties may arise with other employees if they see young men entering the company on comparatively high salaries. This is not usually a problem if the position and capacity of the business graduate are commensurate with his salary. He should not be paid more for the same work than anyone else. Problems arise more frequently when a business graduate holds a position higher than men many years his senior. In such a situation the business graduate has to convince subordinates personally of his ability and qualifications for the job. This requires a high level of interpersonal skills to match his technical skills.

The above remarks apply both to the graduate fresh out of business school and to the graduate with subsequent experience. In the case of the latter his experience and achievement after business school must carry weight with the potential employer. However, it should be remembered that the business graduate is highly adaptable and while his experience may be in a different area, what counts is the degree of success he has achieved. In the case of the graduate fresh out of business school, his prior experience is usually less important than his business school training. However, pertinent questions should be asked about his earlier career and reasons for going to business school.

PLACEMENT

Once a company has decided to investigate the business graduate with a view to filling various positions in the organisation, it frequently finds it difficult to know how to proceed. In the case of people just graduating from business school, the schools themselves offer placement services which vary from the excellent to the inadequate, and the names of the placement officers have been given in the *Guide* where these have been available. The role of the placement officer is not merely to act as a clearing house for job opportunities, but also to meet employers, discuss in what ways a business graduate could help them and assist them in defining the specific skills required. Particularly in the case of the company entering the business graduate market for the first time, such discussions can be of considerable assistance in facilitating both the process of recruitment and the subsequent integration of the business graduate.

The major American schools also provide class profiles for their graduating classes, in the form of collected curriculum vitae. This practice has not yet spread far in the United Kingdom. It enables employers to contact students direct, with the possible disadvantage that most employers make offers to the best qualified who are often over-qualified for the majority of positions offered. In the United Kingdom it is more common for the schools to collate the various offers of employment and allow the students to apply individually. Under this system the employer should state his precise requirements, as relatively undefined job specifications tend to attract a plethora of enquiries which makes the selection process long drawn out and in consequence, expensive. Many schools organise the "milk round" by which employers are given facilities on the premises to interview students.

In the case of recruitment of business graduates of several years standing the means of approach are less well-defined. It is possible to reach both this group and new business graduates via press advertising, though this usually means paying for a blanket coverage well in excess of the target population. The various firms of executive employment brokers, the "head-hunters", have a certain amount of experience in the recruitment of business graduates and probably can pinpoint effective media in reaching specific targets. The Business Graduates Association has a system of circularising employment opportunities to its members, which is a very economical means of reaching a large proportion of business graduates. One of the BGA's aims is the effective employment of the business graduate and it is therefore always willing to assist employers wherever possible with up-to-date information.

The question of pay is frequently a vexed issue. If business graduates are employed at levels that reflect their talents and qualifications, this brings their salaries into perspective, and the business graduate is then frequently seen as something of a bargain. Relative to his age group, the business graduate asks for and usually gets a salary premium, but this merely reflects an additional array of talents developed by business education. It must be remembered that business graduates have frequently made a big investment in their education in terms of direct outlay and salary foregone while at business school and therefore expect a reasonable rate of return on this investment. Employers should beware of average salaries quoted for business school graduates as these conceal a considerable range; they may well be able to recruit young but highly able staff at a rather lower rate, or they may have to pay rather more for those with particularly good qualifications and considerable pre-business school experience in the relevant area. The employer will usually also find that business graduates are prepared for some fairly hard bargaining over salaries. This has alarmed some employers, but most recognise that it is far better to hammer out substantive issues prior to the commencement of employment rather than have to deal with them on the job.

JOB AVAILABILITY

What kind of jobs do new business graduates tend to obtain? Much research on employment patterns has been carried out by the BGA and others and one or two surprising conclusions can be stated.

New busness graduates with little business experience prior to business school, and even those who have some experience, can expect their first jobs after business school to be in a staff position. These posts are generally advisory, requiring the skills of data collection, analysis and generation of conclusions and recommendations. They can be associated with any traditional functional area, and are often associated with some central planning or advisory service. Many graduates with previous experience find excellent first employment opportunities in management consultancy operations, whether internal departments of large manufacturing firms or in specialised consultancy firms. Similarly, those with additional professional accounting qualifications can obtain some well paid jobs in industry, banking or consultancy, but such persons would tend to be older and more experienced than most.

First line management posts can be expected after a year or two assuming that the business graduate has proved himself. Some prefer to stay on in staff positions and obviously for the consultant who begins to play more responsible roles in projects, the continual contact with a variety of client organisations throws up many job opportunities.

Research shows that all kinds of firms and industries are recruiting business graduates. A majority go into manufacturing industry, and significant proportions go into banking and other financial organisations and also management consultancy. More business graduates are going into teaching and a proportion go back to family firms or even found their own.

As the business graduate's career progresses, two distinct trends are seen. The first, which is to be expected and is confirmed by research, is that business graduates tend to move fairly rapidly into general management positions. The other, and perhaps more interesting trend, is the one showing business graduates moving into smaller firms as their careers advance. This trend may reflect nothing more than the possibility that more general management posts are available in smaller firms merely because there are more such firms than large ones. It is also true that many people find more responsibility at an earlier age in small firms and more enjoyment in working in them. The figures also reflect the fact that a proportion of business graduates start their own businesses.

Until the middle 1970s, lack of understanding of the new phenomenon gave rise in the UK and Europe to controversy over the employment of business graduates. This has now been followed by the realisation that the business graduate is just another employee, but one whose special qualifications justify special care in his selection and use. Companies who have done this confirm that he is outstanding value for money.

CHAPTER 4

The Prospective Student

For the benefit of those who have had little or no prior contact with business schools or their graduates, it is worth reiterating that the skills and knowledge covered in a business course are applicable to all forms of organisation and that it is not necessary to have entrepreneurial ambitions to find a business course useful. This should not deter potential entrepreneurs, however. Business schools, having become rather more self-confident, are now trying to attract a wider variety of students, and this must improve the breadth of the course and give students wider opportunities for subjecting their views to possible hostile scrutiny. This reflects the fact that in the last few years the commercial world has become much more open and is actively seeking new ideas. Business graduates find that they are actively recruited for situations of change, to engineer change within organisations, and to generate new thinking on objectives and structures.

The foregoing suggests that the principal reason for going to business school is the prospect of a subsequent job with more interest and responsibility than one might otherwise have had. The salary prospects are also undeniably attractive to most people. It is undoubtedly important to have thought hard about ambitions and opportunities and to have considered whether they are consistent with one's personality and personal talents. This process of introspective analysis is most important and most difficult. For many, the decision to go to business school involves considerable financial stringency, as many students have to finance themselves in some way and suffer loss of earnings whilst away from a job. The disruption to family life, if the student is married, must be borne in mind as the student in most business schools has to work extremely hard if he wishes to pass well. So the individual considering going to business school must be pretty clear about the way he wishes his life to develop, and that he is capable intellectually, emotionally and in other ways of successfully completing the business school programme.

Having identified a set of personal objectives before going to business school, few people emerge with the same set of goals and attitudes which they had on entry. The effect of the exposure to a wide variety of other people and the immense broadening of horizons brought about by this and by the course content and teaching, make most students evalute both their goals and themselves in a new light. Indeed, many have commented that they did not really know what an objective was before their business school course.

It must be reiterated that the course is not a guarantee of future wealth, fame or responsibility. Only the individual, through achievement, opens such doors. As soon as business school becomes a low-risk option it must lose a great deal of its effectiveness and become much less attractive to the sort of students and employers it wishes to attract. While, therefore, the prospective student should carefully analyse the external factors (the opportunities open at the present time, his ambitions and their consonance with his opportunities), he should also be motivated by the educational process itself, and the prospect of being able to realise his personal educational development, and this will remain true until the concept of continuous adult education is established. The student is likely to have at least thirty years future employment before him, and we can be certain that the world in the early 2000s will be faced by problems of which we are only vaguely, if at all, aware.

The vista of rapid change means that the recent phenomenon of the redundant manager is unlikely to disappear and that the most valuable employees will be those who have had training and education which will enable them to adjust to new roles and skills. Meritocracy is alive and well.

If the image of business schools presented herein appeals, then the next question is, "When is the best time to go?" There can be no definite answer to this, as it depends heavily on the individual and his situation. Lack of experience is frequently a problem and not merely one with new graduates. Frequently technologists find that though they have been employed for a few years or more, the nature of their employment experience has not differed markedly from their previous educational training. Indeed, business education seems to many to be the means of escape from a narrow employment environment. Geographical location and post mobility can also have a major bearing on the relevance and depth of experience of the individual. The more experienced he is, the easier it will be for him to fit the course material into a coherent framework. However, there is a trade-off between this and other factors. It becomes progressively more difficult to learn and re-adapt to study as one gets older; also personal and financial commitments accumulate and may make a course difficult to pursue. Many feel that the opportunity is worth taking, if it is offered, as it may never recur, but careful thought should be given to whether one has sufficient knowledge and experience to make the course worthwhile.

This does not mean that the new graduate does not fit in. Many people undertake a wide range of vacation employment while studying for a first degree and become involved in running clubs, societies, etc.; this is sometimes an adequate proxy for subsequent experience. Also the new graduate frequently brings a rather less conditioned attitude and brand of criticism to the school. He should, however, aim for a school which takes less than 50 per cent new graduates at the outside, as the dialogue with those with greater experience is of great value.

If business school education seems appropriate at the present stage of one's career, there is then the problem of choosing a school. This decision is particularly important in view of the potentially large sums of money involved and possible differing impact on one's future career patterns. There is no one ideal course or learning method, as individuals naturally have differing objectives, cultural values and learning patterns, and while all schools welcome a wide variety of students, there can be mismatches, leading to difficulties for the student. It is, therefore, vital to relate opportunities to present objectives, values and expectations. While a business school course will probably change these, it is important to avoid rapid disillusionment by making sure to relate them to the course. Discussion with others is a valuable aid in this respect. It is also essential to choose courses which match one's abilities. For an over-qualified student, the course is merely another paper qualification. On the other hand, an under-qualified person may be overstressed and fail at the end of the course.

A further source of stress in business school courses can be financial difficulties. It is unwise to budget for the bare minimum, as the course is certain to be at high pressure. This means that relaxation is all the more necessary, however rare it may be, and also, as has already been stated, the social aspect of the course is important. It cannot be too much emphasised that money worries have a most harmful effect on both course performance and personal relationships.

WHICH TYPE OF COURSE?

The classic differentiation of courses is between specialist and generalist ones. With the development of business education this is now less a dichotomy than a continuous spectrum. The choice here is dependent upon long-term or short-term career objectives and personal capacity.

The generalist course

This is the archetypal business school course leading to the degree of Master of Business Administration, the MBA, or its equivalent and provides a foundation in a broad range of business skills designed for a long-term career in general management. It is of most relevance to those who are potential senior managers as much of the course training relates to policy decisions and the setting of organisation objectives.

The generalist course with a specialist option

While most MBA degrees include a significant number of specialist options, the graduate is not normally labelled according to choice of option. Nevertheless, there are an increasing number of courses where a major option is included, such as Marketing or Finance, as a result of which the graduate can also claim to be a specialist in that field, and enter employment as such, moving into general management later. For the graduate with little or no prior experience it can be an easier way of making the transition to permanent employment, while retaining long-term prospects of general management.

The specialist course

Here the course contains little outside the specialist area, so that the graduate subsequently becomes a professional in a specific business field. As his skills are more specific the openings into general management tend to be correspondingly fewer.

WHERE?

Unlike many other areas of education, potential business school students around the world can legitimately ask the question, "Which country shall I study in?" The traditional location was North America where business schools have been operating for half a century. But in the last decade schools of international repute have opened their doors in Britain and France and increasingly in other countries around the world. Consequently, Australia, Israel, South Africa, Spain and other countries possess excellent institutions which will surely gain more influence and reputation over the coming years.

The following comments are of necessity generalisations, and there is a wide range of variation between schools in each geographic area.

North America

The basic United States pattern of higher education is for a number

22

of self-contained modular courses to be taken each term and for these to be assessed on the basis of written work, possible class participation, and examinations at the end of term. The aggregate of course grades received determines the quality of the final degree. This system means that students have to adhere to a structured programme of work in each course. This is offset, however, by a wide choice of courses and considerable flexibility in choices. It means that it is hard to pursue points of interest outside the course to the depth one might desire, and it leads to continuous pressure being maintained throughout the term. The cost of going to a United States school must also be considered, as even if a financial award is obtained, these do not generally cover more than a proportion of outgoings. The same may .be said of Canadian schools, though the cost is markedly less and finance is often more easily obtained.

Europe
Though English is acceptable for IMEDE (the Management Development Institute), French is necessary for INSEAD (European Institute of Business Administration) and German is useful. This last school insists on fluent French, without which it would be difficult to follow the course and communicate with many fellow students. Assessment and course structure follow the American model though the programmes take nine months as opposed to the two-year United States norm. The cost is somewhat less than going to the USA, but considerably more than for study in the United Kingdom. The advantage of the European schools is their geographically widely spread "old boy network" and a possible disadvantage is their isolation from the rest of the higher educational system.

United Kingdom
The variety and quality of business education in the United Kingdom compares favourably even with the USA. In general, the United Kingdom schools have major examinations at the end of the programme, usually coupled with a dissertation or thesis to form the bulk of the performance assessment. Some schools, notably London, combine this with continuous assessment on the American pattern. Finance is considerably easier to obtain here, and even financing oneself costs much less than going abroad. Class sizes are frequently smaller than elsewhere which leads to closer links between faculty and students, at the possible expense of a less heterogeneous student body.

Except for the part-time MBA which is not yet widespread in the United Kingdom, the choice is basically between nine-month, twelve-month, and two-year courses. Twelve-month courses are generally similar to nine-month ones, with the addition of a project lasting three months. The longer two-year course is not necessarily less intensive than the shorter ones, but does tend to give more time for exploration of areas of interest. Many people, especially after the age of thirty, feel that it is better to minimise the time away from business and therefore prefer the shorter course, whereas others find that one year is not long enough to take full advantage of the opportunities offered.

This must necessarily be a matter for the individual to decide. The shorter courses result in a lesser loss of earnings and a lower total cost, which may be significant in the context of family expenses and mortgage repayments. However, as has been pointed out before, while finance is obviously a limiting factor, it should not be the primary factor in the decision. Some firms feel that the two-year course is significantly more useful.

ENTRY QUALIFICATIONS

Most schools require a degree or a professional equivalent as a prime entry requirement. What constitutes an acceptable professional equivalent is rarely well defined. Professional accounting qualifications (ACA, ACCA and ACMA) are frequently accepted, as surveys show, so the answer is to apply and, especially in North America, to persevere and not take no for an answer. Some schools are prepared to take managers without any formal tertiary qualification but who can demonstrate significant experience in a position of responsibility and the intellectual ability to deal with the course in question. Again it is worth trying if one is not sure. Certain courses in specialised areas define the required content of the first degree or equivalent qualifications. On the other hand, when a school requires some acquaintance with mathematics, this should not deter arts and other non- or semi-numerate graduates from applying, as one can usually cover the material by directed study beforehand. There are however several basic requirements in the United Kingdom for United Kingdom students; these usually take the form of a requirement that the student has passed "O" Level or equivalent in Mathematics and English. Almost all schools, not only those in North America, will require applicants to take the "Graduate Management Admission Test" formerly known to many as the "Princeton Test". This test is administered by the Graduate Management Admission Council, Educational Testing Service of Princeton, New Jersey (see p. 29). Many North American schools require candidates whose native language is not English to take the "Test of English as a Foreign Language" (TOEFL). TOEFL is also administered by the Educational Testing Service.

COMPILING A SHORT-LIST

With careful consideration one should be able to draw up a short-list of about half a dozen courses which appear suitable and then to write off for a prospectus and application form from each. Armed with such additional information as the prospectus can provide, it is then worth-while if possible discussing such facts as faculty quality with recent graduates from the schools in question. The BGA runs seminars and counselling sessions to advise people in these matters and details of the next seminar and of any other sources of information may be obtained from the BGA offices.

It is important to make sure that particular subjects of interest are catered for within the context of the various courses and the less numerate graduate should make sure he obtains some mathematical and statistical training as these are playing a major role in management today. Similarly, those with a mathematical background should aim to broaden their experience in other areas. Also there are areas which few go to business school with the intention of studying in depth yet find very useful in their subsequent careers. Behavioural science, under its many names, and computing are examples. Brochures being notoriously deceptive, one should ascertain whether the faculty is capable of teaching the courses offered.

Another factor which should be considered in ranking different schools is their geographical location. Proximity to centres of industrial or commercial activity may facilitate contacts with the business world. Suitable accommodation at a reasonable price has to be found for the student and possibly his family. Living too far from the school can hinder contact with fellow students and even course participation. A high-pressure course can leave very little leisure time so it is important to remember that a married student's wife may find herself effectively on her own in a strange town. If married accommodation is available on the campus this can significantly reduce the personal problems which might arise.

CHAPTER 5

How to Apply

Many business schools set an application deadline around March for entry in the following September, and accept applications from about the previous October. This emphasises the need to be planning at least one year in advance: the earlier one applies and gets a decision the longer time there is available to choose between several offers and to make the necessary financial and personal arrangements. Earlier applicants are also likely to find it easier to obtain funds from various sources. It should be also borne in mind that many scholarships have application deadlines.

The aim should therefore be, particularly if one wishes to study abroad, to have gathered the necessary information and submitted application by Christmas at the latest. However, where no specific application deadlines are stated it is usually possible to be accepted right up to the beginning of the academic year, especially in the cases of self-financed students and the less popular schools.

In the case of United States schools there is now usually an application fee of around $30. This must accompany the application form and is used to defray processing costs. It is not returnable, nor can it be set against any other fees incurred. This emphasises the selection process the prospective student must go through before applying to business schools: applying to many will be an expensive pastime. Again, in the case of United States schools, details are usually given in the prospectus of the schedule for processing applications. In general, these mean that the time between the reception of an application and the notification is about two months.

The following are major criteria used in the selection of students by business schools. The actual criteria and the weighting used by the schools in question are laid out in the *Guide*.

THE APPLICATION FORM

The application form should not be taken lightly. Indeed, in many cases the form will not allow itself to be taken lightly. It is not just an academic and business career record, but also requires the applicant to give quite lengthy answers to questions such as: "Please give a frank impression of your own character indicating what you believe to be your major strengths and weaknesses."; "What do you consider to be your most significant achievement to date?"; "Why is it significant to you?"; "What do you feel that you personally could contribute to the department and to your fellow students?"; "Discuss the career opportunities which you consider are open to you at the present time"; "Outline on a separate sheet a statement of your purpose in pursuing the degree for which you are applying including current objectives and career goals."

The applicant is expected to sell himself and provide a reasonable account of his ambitions and career to date. This should not be overdone, however, as these accounts will be compared with the references that are also required. It is useful to write the answer out in rough first and get one's wife, a close friend, or a colleague to comment of them. It is very easy to sound trite or priggish in this sort of exercise. Having achieved a reasonable final version, which can be used with modification on most application forms, the application form itself should then be typed unless it specifically states the contrary – if so, this may indicate some form of handwriting analysis, which has been used before, in processing application forms. Incidentally, for many the filling out of an application form for an American school will be the first contact they have with American bureaucracy. Not only will they find standard questions of the "Why do you want an MBA?" and "What makes you think we should accept you?" type, but also affidavits concerning your financial status signed by Notaries Public will be required together with exhortations to take "The Tests". These include GMAT (Graduate Management Admission Test – the Princeton Test) and TOEFL (Test of English as a Foreign Language). Also may be found questions concerning one's ethnic origin (American Indian, Alaskan Native, Black-non-Hispanic, Asian or Pacific Islander, Hispanic, Caucasian, non-Hispanic). Such questions are "used only for affirmative action reporting purposes". These statements are usually accompanied by a paragraph similar to the following; that the University "reaffirms its policy that discrimination on the basis of race, color, religion, national origin, sex, sex orientation, handicap or age will not be practised in any of its activities. Complaints and issues surrounding the implementation of this policy should be addressed to the Affirmative Action Co-ordinator, Office of the University

Commitment to Human Resources", etc. As with most things the Americans embrace bureaucracy with zest and thoroughness.

REFERENCES

These are not universally required but it is normal for the applicant to get two referees to submit references on forms that usually accompany the application form. They frequently ask for comments on the relationship of the applicant with fellow students, colleagues, or superiors. A certain amount of thought should go into choosing referees and they should then be given either prior warning or a reasonable time to complete the reference as these may take some time. For graduates, a reference from the head of one's undergraduate department or a senior member of staff will be required and a second reference from either another member of the college staff, or a present or previous employer. For those with professional qualifications two employers' references will be required, possibly including the one under whom one gained the qualification. There are some obvious pitfalls to avoid: some academics and some employers may be suspicious of business education; also, unless one is sponsored by one's present employer, a certain amount of acrimony may creep into the reference. Problems do not usually arise, but references are not disclosed to applicants and a little forethought may pay dividends.

ACADEMIC RECORD

Details of one's academic career have to be included on the application form and further information may be required of referees. It is also almost universal practice to request certificates for verification at some time before entry. The school will be looking for some evidence of intellectual ability and it will compare academic results with one's GMAT score. A good honours degree is useful but not essential, as a good GMAT score can make up a lower degree class. Most schools require a level of mathematics up to "O" Level standard; some schools require more. North American schools normally request official transcripts of academic records from all colleges, universities or professional schools the applicant has attended.

EMPLOYMENT EXPERIENCE

After a few years work this is just as important as previous academic achievements. Some schools consider managers without a degree or professional qualification if they have a wide enough experience and can demonstrate sufficient intellectual ability. Many schools are remarkably flexible if one perseveres. What schools are interested in is less the type of employment, than that the applicant should have been reasonably successful. It is not in a school's interest to become a refuge from employment. Width of experience is also particularly important and should not be underplayed on the application form unless departures from jobs have been involuntary!

INTERVIEWS

These are rarely used as a prime selection mechanism and indeed are quite often not required at all, particularly in the USA. They do, however, help the applicant's decision in that he can meet some of the faculty and go round the school. Even if an interview is not required, if it is possible to attend it is worth asking for one for the purpose of information. It is after all somewhat foolhardy to bank one's future on somewhere one has never seen. Some United Kingdom schools run selection conferences where a large group of applicants visit the business school together and meet staff and existing students and subsequently have a short interview. The interviewer will be looking to fill out and confirm the image gained from the application form. Interviewers look for different things in applicants (standards vary whenever more than one person operates the selection process), but a prime factor is the ability to communicate verbally. Appearance is likely to have some subconscious impact on the interviewer; after all, they will have to market the student at the end of the course. Simulation or dissimulation are ill-advised, as the stereo-type of the business graduate never was accurate and schools are now consciously striving for a more widely-based and pluralistic student body.

TESTS

Graduate Management Admission Test

This test, previously known as the Princeton Test, is sponsored and controlled by the Graduate Management Admissions Council, consisting of representatives of forty-eight graduate business schools. The Education Testing Service of Princeton, New Jersey, administers the test and a 65-page booklet describing how to take the test is sent free with the registration form to all enquirers. The address is: GMAT, Fulbright Commission, 6 Porter Street, London W1M 2HR. Tel: (01) 486 1098. Enclose 13 × 9 inches envelope stamped for 100 grams. Those living outside the UK should apply to the nearest US Embassy.

Most American schools and a number of British schools require applicants to take the GMAT and they use the scores as one of their selection criteria. The test, which last three and a half hours, measures ability to read, understand and reason logically in both verbal and quantitative terms. Those who take the test are neither required nor expected to have had undergraduate preparation in business subjects. However, the comprehension passages tend to be taken from business or economic journals and some practice in reading these is well worthwhile to become familiar with the style of questions. This is particularly important for those not familiar with United States-type tests. Candidates from a United Kingdom background, for example, usually score less than the equivalent United States candidates. Candidates whose first language is not English tend to be at a disadvantage. However, business schools take these factors into account when evaluating the score with the application. Registration forms should be returned at least six weeks before the test date, together with the test fee.

The GMAT booklet contains a few sample questions, and two review books (written by E.C. Gruber) are published in the USA; one by Arco and one by Simon and Schuster. Another company offers a complete trial test and a service which calculates your score and percentile rank just like the official test. This has a United Kingdom office and the address to write to is PasTest Service, P.O. Box 81, Hemel Hempstead, Herts. Tel: (0442) 52113.

Sittings of the test are arranged four times a year at foreign centres, normally in November, February, April and June. All candidates are advised to take the GMAT as early as possible. Since many business schools make their admissions decisions in the Spring, February test scores are often the latest they can consider. There is no pass-mark on the GMAT but applicants can judge their chances of success from the test score. The average for graduates is about 500 and the major schools take few people below 550. In the case of certain major business schools, the absolute cut-off point is 450. However, the United States orientation of the test is taken into account in the evaluation of an applicant's test score. A reasonable balance between the quantitative and verbal scores is also desirable. While the top business schools may have a mean score in the low to mid-600s (the perfect score is 800), this does not mean they automatically take high scores, nor that they eliminate lower scores. The test is not a dominant selection criterion and admissions committees look as much for prior achievement, at university and at work, and at the applicant's level of motivation and commitment. While a certain amount of practice is valuable, repetition of the test is by no means guaranteed to improve one's score. It appears that at least one-third of those retaking the test actually score lower at the second attempt. As prior scores may well be in the possession of business schools (through earlier applications), retaking the test is generally only advisable where there are definite reasons for assuming that one's performance was impaired. Presented with a significant record of achievement both at university and at work, most business schools will accept that the GMAT score may merely reflect an "off" day.

Other tests

There are various tests used for applicants whose first language is not English. Details of requirements are available either in the prospectus or by enquiry from the schools concerned. One such test constantly referred to is another by the Education Testing Service, Princeton, New Jersey. It is referred to as TOEFL or Test of English as a Foreign Language. Applicants for courses with a high content of non-business studies subjects may be required to take, instead of GMAT, the GRE or Graduate Record Examination. This comes in two parts, an aptitude test plus an advanced test geared to a specific subject area. Again the organisation to contact is the Educational Testing Service. Applicants attending selection conferences at other schools may be asked to complete short mathematical tests, vocational tests, or character profiles, though the use of these is limited.

CHAPTER 6

Finance and Personal Arrangements

FINANCE

Probably the most important question for many prospective business students is how to obtain sufficient funds for the course, particularly if one wishes to study abroad or has family commitments.

The *Guide* gives the cost of tuition for the majority of schools and also an estimate of the annual cost to the student. This varies somewhat according to whether it was calculated on the basis of the academic year or a full calendar year. The estimates are of course for a single person. A married student with no children would need about 25 per cent more in the United States and in the United Kingdom, where the cost of tuition is a smaller proportion of the total estimate, possibly 50 per cent more. Given the recent fluctuations of exchange rates, fees and cost estimates have been left in the currency of the country concerned.

It is important to make sure that one has earmarked sufficient funds to cover the course adequately. Financial worries can cause severe problems especially on a high-intensity course. While one may live fairly frugally during the course it is essential to have sufficient funds for books, for example. As a significant part of the benefit of the course comes from contact with one's fellow students one also needs to budget for a certain amount of social expenditure.

All the possible sources of funds should be explored at an early stage. The following list gives sources which have been used to wholly or partially finance a business course:

(*a*) company sponsorship;
(*b*) grants or bursaries;
(*c*) open scholarships;
(*d*) college scholarships;
(*e*) loans;
(*f*) personal savings or private income;

32

(g) family assistance and spouse's earnings;

(h) part-time and vacation work.

Company sponsorship

Some companies, Ford for example, send a number of employees to business schools as sponsored students as a matter of routine, and there is a fairly standardised procedure of nomination of candidates. In other companies where there may be few, if any, precedents, the prospective business school student has to take the initiative in proposing possible sponsorship to the employer. It is extremely rare for companies to sponsor people other than current employees on a post-graduate programme, though this should not deter the new graduate, for example, approaching companies. The arrangements vary considerably, and it is possible for the company to utilise the Industrial Training Grants system in offering sponsorship, which can markedly reduce the effective cost to the company. Normally, a sponsored student would be paid his fees plus reasonable living expenses, sometimes even full salary, and be expected to work for the employer for about two years at the end of the course and probably also in the long vacation of a two-year course. The pecuniary advantages of sponsorhip during the course are evident, but there are drawbacks and caution should be exercised in accepting an offer. It is easier to iron out potential problems beforehand than after. The first difficulty is that the sponsored student may not be promoted on his return to the organisation and thus may see his post-business school salary being markedly lower than those of his fellow graduates. If on the other hand he is promoted rapidly, his erstwhile colleagues in the firm are apt to regard him with suspicion. Some people find their objectives change while they are at business school and find the requirement of remaining with the company a brake on their career. Finally, when he returns it is by no means uncommon for the company to have no idea what to do with him, which leads to dissatisfaction on both sides.

Grants

(a) The Economical and Social Research Council (ESRC) and the Science and Engineering Research Council are the largest single sources of finance for post-graduate business education in the United Kingdom. The Science and Engineering Research Council's interest in this area is limited to courses with a high quantitative or scientific content, but the following remarks, in general, apply to it as well as the ESRC.

There are two types of award given by the ESRC to students on approved courses; studentships for those courses of study leading to a higher degree, and bursaries for postgraduate diploma or certificate work. These differ in that bursaries are liable to parental contributions like undergraduate grants unless the student is over twenty-five, or has three years employment experience, or is a married woman over twenty-one, whereas studentships are not subject to parental contributions. Studentships are divided into "quota" and "pool" awards. Some approved courses are allocated a number of awards for them to distribute as they see fit to eligible students, which are "quota" awards; students on these courses are also eligible to compete with students on the other approved courses for "pool" awards, which are allocated on an open basis. Applications are not made directly to the ESRC but are made through the institution concerned. ESRC awards cover tuition fees, plus a maintenance grant based on a thirty week academic year. These grants start at £1,530 for a student living at home, to £2,950 for students in London away from home. Additional allowances are available to older students ranging from an additional £450 for a student at twenty-two to £1,350 for one twenty-seven years old or over. Allowances of up to £600 are paid for each child under eleven and up to £1,120 for other dependents not working. (These rates are for 1984 and are revised each year.) Outside income ought to be deducted from the award. Queries about awards should be directed to the ESRC, as these figures are correct only at the time of writing. A booklet of information on either the studentship or the bursary regulations is sent by the school to the student with the necessary application forms but copies may also be obtained by writing to: The Pre-Awards Section, Economics and Social Research Council, 1 Temple Avenue, London EC4Y 0BD.

(b) *Other grants.* The Foundation for Management Education gives bursaries to business school students in the United Kingdom. The bursaries are all allocated by the schools themselves and are subject to similar regulations to ESRC bursaries. Like ESRC grants they can only be applied for through the school itself.

The Manpower Services Commission has for some years been sponsoring experienced students on Business School courses. Normally such sponsorship is received for redundant executives who it is felt would be able to find a job more easily having obtained such advanced training. Policies are seemingly constantly under review and advice should be sought from the local office of the Commission.

Open scholarships

These are scholarships which are available for more than one school and whose allocation is decided by competition. They are of interest to those wishing to study abroad. They are not always sufficient to cover full maintenance or fees. The following list is probably by no means complete, as there are no doubt other sources of educational funds which might be available for business school education.

FINANCE AND PERSONAL ARRANGEMENTS

(a) *Charles R.E. Bell Fund.* Available for study in the USA. Details from: London Chamber of Commerce, 69 Cannon Street, London EC4. Tel: (01) 248 4444

(b) *Commonwealth Scholarships.* These are available for study in any Commonwealth country other than the one in which one is resident. It is therefore of interest to students wishing to go to Canada. It is a condition of these awards that scholars must return to their own country on the completion of the course. Prospectus and application form from: The Joint Secretaries, Commonwealth Scholarships Commission in the United Kingdom, 36 Gordon Square, London WC1M 0PF. Tel: (01) 387 8572

(c) *English Speaking Union.* Graduate Assistantships at certain United States Universities. Details from: The English Speaking Union of the Commonwealth, 37 Charles Street, London W1. Tel: (01) 629 8995

(d) *Harkness Fellowships.* Tenable in the USA. Details from: Harkness House, 38 Upper Brook Street, London W1. Tel: (01) 629 2232

(e) *Kennedy Scholarships.* Tenable at Harvard and MIT. Details from: The Kennedy Memorial Fund, Association of Commonwealth Universities, 36 Gordon Square, London WC1M 0PF. Tel: (01) 387 8572

(f) *Rotary Foundation Fellowships for International Understanding.* Details from: Rotary International in Great Britain and Ireland, Sheen Lane House, Sheen Lane, London SW14. Tel: (01) 878 0931

Other similar sources include: National Association of Foreign Student Affairs, 1860 19th St. N.W., Washington, D.C. 20009; Organization of American States, 17th & Constitution Ave. N.W., Washington, D.C. 20006; The International Institute of Education, 809 United Nations Plaza, New York, New York 10017; The Latin American Scholarship Program of American Universities, 25 Mt. Auburn St., Cambridge, Mass. 02138; American Friends of the Middle East, 1717 Massachusetts Ave., Washington, D.C. 20009; African American Institute, 866 United Nations Plaza, New York, New York 10017; and the Committee of International Exchange of Scholars, 2101 Constitution Ave., Washington, D.C. 20418. It is possible that some of these organisations have offices in the applicant's country. The applicant should contact that office, or write to the address above.

There are many publications relating to financial assistance which should be consulted. Publications can be found in United States Information Service (USIS) libraries (usually located in a country's capital city); in Institute of International Education offices in Hong Kong, Bangkok, Lima, Nairobi, and Mexico City; and in US libraries. Finally, funding possibilities should be explored through the last academic institution the applicant attended.

College scholarships
In the United Kingdom scholarships play a very minor part in the financing of business school students. In the United States, however, a larger number of scholarships are available. Only a proportion of these are open for foreign competition; details and conditions are usually given in the prospectus. It should be noted that these very rarely cover more than a proportion of the total cost, so while they may be valuable assistance they are not sufficient on their own. Applications are made through the school with the following exceptions.

(a) *Thouron Awards*. Twenty-five awards are available annually in any division of the University of Pennsylvania. They are thus available for Wharton, and cover maintenance and fees. Details from: The Office of the Registrar (Thouron Awards), University of Glasgow, Glasgow W2 Scotland.

(b) *Frank Knox Fellowships*. These are tenable at Harvard and cover fees plus a substantial proportion of maintenance costs. Details from: Frank Knox Fellowships, Association of Commonwealth Universities, 36 Gordon Square, London WC1M 0PF.

Loans
In the United States a substantial amount of loan finance is available and details can be found in the various hand books and prospectuses. However, it may not be available to foreign students. Repayments may be a difficulty if they are to be paid from a United Kingdom post-business school salary. However, certain business schools, e.g. Harvard, operate a special repayment scheme for United Kingdom based graduates.

All these schemes are subsidised or endowed in some way. The current high rates of interest make commercial loan finance distinctly unattractive at the present time, were it even readily available. In the United Kingdom a number of loan schemes operate through business schools, notably those of the BGA and the Conference of University Management Schools. Enquiries to the school concerned will reveal whether the course has loan finance available and this has been indicated as far as is possible in the *Guide*.

The BGA scheme is restricted to business courses on the BGA list (*see* Appendix II) and offers loans at very favourable rates of interest over a fairly extended repayment period. Applicants must, in general, have had two years' business experience and may apply any time after acceptance via the school principal, for schools in the UK or direct to the National Westminster Bank, Lloyds and Barclays for foreign schools. The maximum amount available per annum is

£3,000 plus fees or two-thirds of previous salary, whichever is the greater for UK schools, £12,000 for foreign schools (which may be increased at the bank's discretion). Other major clearing banks operate loan schemes either through the BGA or direct. Loans need not be the sole method of finance, indeed many of the applicants use a medium-size loan to supplement grants, particularly if they have financial commitments of a substantial nature. Details of the BGA scheme are given in Appendix IV.

Personal saving or private income
Very few people can wholly support themselves while at business school; nevertheless, personal savings are a useful way of eking out other finances. As one is planning, hopefully, twelve months ahead for business school entry, it is worth starting to save fairly systematically as soon as possible.

Family assistance and spouse's earnings
While one may be reluctant to accept or borrow money from other members of one's family, frequently parents or relatives are more than ready to contribute. However, it is more likely that a prospective student is married and hopes to count on the financial support of the wife or husband. In the United Kingdom it is of course relatively easy to check on the employment possibilities and wives with a skill like typing, for example, should have no difficulty finding employment. On the Continent, while there should be no problems with work permits etc., it will probably be difficult to find employment for one's wife, especially if she is not reasonably bilingual. In the USA employment opportunities differ markedly from place to place and if at all possible a job should be arranged in advance. This may well complicate visa arrangements. Many United States universities, however, have bureaux which arrange the employment of wives or husbands within the university. If such an arrangement exists, details are usually included in the prospectus, but it is worth specifically enquiring when writing.

Part-time or vacation work
On most two-year courses the student is expected to spend the long vacation in the middle engaged on a paid project in business. This employment may have to be found by the student, or alternatively the school may give some assistance in finding projects and employers. Sponsored students usually return to their own company for the period. The long vacation therefore should at least cover living expenses for the period and one may manage to save for some of the subsequent year. Employment in the other vacations, which are usually little more than a fortnight, is hard to find, unless it is on a

freelance basis in something like computer programming, or such hardy perennials as the Post Office Christmas work.

The Continental schools offer shorter courses which leave little opportunity in them for outside activity. In North America, however, there are substantial opportunities for both part-time and vacation work. One should ensure in advance if one intends working in the United States that one gets the right visa. It may be difficult to obtain a visa that will enable one to work in the United States and this should be investigated early on in the application process. As well as work in the long vacation, there are various part-time jobs such as Research and Teaching Assistantships available that make modest demands on one's time and can cover a large proportion, if not all, of one's expenses, as fees are frequently waived for Assistants in the United States. These opportunities are normally only available to doctoral students in the United Kingdom.

PERSONAL ARRANGEMENTS

Accommodation
Most schools have accommodation available for a proportion of their students. This is more commonly for unmarried students and in the United States it is likely that they will have to share a room. In the United Kingdom the vast majority of student accommodation is in single rooms. In both cases the earlier one applies the more likely one is to get allocated accommodation particularly in the case of married students. Even if the school does not provide accommodation there is frequently a bureau attached to the University which offers assistance in finding rooms. Most of those who have dealt with these bureaux recommend that one perseveres until suitable accommodation is obtained. It is important to try and live within reasonably easy reach of the school in question as this facilitates participation in the course and peripheral activities.

Information for those going to the USA
There is a choice of visas for which one may apply: an "F" Student Visa, which does not permit one to undertake any paid employment; a "J-1" Exchange Visitor Visa, with which one may apply on arrival to the United States Immigration Service for permission to work; or an Immigration Visa. The regulations should be examined very carefully, particularly if one wants to work in the USA during or after the course. Travel to the United States can be remarkably cheap compared with what it was a few years ago. Rates are changing so frequently that the best advice is to consult your local travel agent.

FURTHER INFORMATION

Detailed information about particular courses, scholarships or local accommodation should be obtained directly from the school concerned. The BGA maintains close links with CUMS (the Conference of University Management Schools), the CNAA (the Council for National Academic Awards) and various other bodies here and overseas, to monitor developments in business courses. Information about the services offered by the Association and details of eligibility to join are available on request to the BGA, 28 Margaret Street, London W1N 7LB. Tel: (01) 637 7611/2.

CHAPTER 7

The Guide

INTRODUCTION

The *Guide to Business Schools* is intended as an initial screening device for prospective students, and for prospective employers of business graduates. From the data included, they can compile a short-list of courses and institutions which they feel may be able to fit their requirements. Further information is available from the schools themselves and should always be sought as it will be up-to-date. The general criterion for a school's inclusion in the *Guide* is that it should offer a postgraduate degree or equivalent in a course relevant to business or management.

The information concerning each school was obtained by the schools themselves filling out a data sheet, an example of which is to be found on p. 41. The data is organised as follows (if for a particular entry a category of data is missing it is probably because the school concerned did not supply it).

THE STRUCTURE OF THE GUIDE

(*a*) *Location of school:* the schools are listed alphabetically by country.

(*b*) *Name of school* or parent institution.

(*c*) *Description:* this attempts to describe the environment in which the school is located, its brief history and amenities.

(*d*) *Admissions Officer:* the person that aspiring students should contact.

(*e*) *Placement Officer:* the person aspiring employers of business graduates should contact.

(*f*) *Graduate Courses offered in Business and Management:* this section gives the names of courses, their duration and enrolment figures for the year 1983/4. There is an attempt to differentiate between that part of a course that is formal classwork and the dissertation or

BGA GUIDE TO BUSINESS SCHOOLS
Schools Data Sheet

Name of School:_____
Location:___ ._____

Brief history (pertinent background information on School):_____

Amenities (local amenities, accommodation and other student facilities, etc.):_____

Admissions Officer:_____

Placement Officer:_____

Graduate Courses offered in Business and Management: Name of Course	Total duration (☐ months), of which: Taught	Dissertation	Enrolments 1979 (No.):
_____	_____	_____	_____
_____	_____	_____	_____
_____	_____	_____	_____
_____	_____	_____	_____

Annual Fees: Citizens_____ Foreign Students _____
Estimated total annual cost to Student 1980/81 (incl. tuition, books, rent, food, etc.): _____

Weighting as an Acceptance Criterion

Admissions criteria:
  Preferred application age range: [_____] _____
  Business experience required: _____ _____%
  Previous formal study/qualification requirements: _____ _____%
  Princeton Test required: YES/NO: Score required: [_____] _____ _____%
  Other criteria: _____ _____%
  _____ _____%
  _____ _____%

Business experience of current class(es): _____

Specialities of the School: _____

Staff numbers — In School: _____
  From other schools teaching on programmes: _____
  From industrial/commercial organisations: [____](Give details of any other links with such organisations): _____

Teaching styles (e.g. case studies, business games, etc.): _____

Assessment criteria and examination frequency: _____

Typical *formal* class hours per week: [_____]
Sources of student finance: _____

Student composition 1979: Foreign students:_____%
                           Women students: _____%
Any other useful data: _____

When completed please return to
The BGA Guide to Business Schools
The Business Graduates Association

41

project that may be required of students after the formal course is completed.

(*g*) *Fees:* most institutions have different fee levels for resident and non-resident students. The definition of resident or non-resident can become difficult, so it pays to enquire most carefully which category you would come into. In some State universities in the USA "foreign" can be defined as out-of-Staters. The figures stated include tuition but may not be the full story as, for example, in the UK, other fees are changing annually so the figures are merely a guide. Those given are for 1984/5, unless otherwise stated.

(*h*) *Admissions criteria:* an attempt to identify the main factors institutions look for and the weighting given to each factor.

(*i*) *Business experience of current student body:* there has always been debate as to the efficacy of doing a Master's course in business without business experience. The benefit to be obtained from attending an institution which has a large proportion of "experienced" students on the course can be of great value. This section tries to highlight the issue.

(*j*) *Specialities of the school:* this section should be treated cautiously – it is an introspective question. Some schools who may not put, say, marketing as a specialty may nevertheless be superior in that area to many other schools.

(*k*) *Staff numbers:* this tries to record two elements, viz. those staff in the school and those "borrowed" from time to time from other schools. Too high a proportion (without trying to define the proportion) of staff servicing from other schools in the institution could suggest that the commitment by the institution to the school is less than ideal, and that many of the staff associated with the course have not the degree of enthusiasm towards the course they would have if it were "their course". It is also interesting to note if any regular contributors to the course are visiting lecturers from industry. This added contact with the real world of business can be most refreshing if done well.

(*l*) *Teaching styles:* most institutions adopt a fairly elastic approach. However if one method is particularly heavily used this is noted.

(*m*) *Assessment criteria and examination frequency:* many different types of assessment methods are adopted though examinations still figure largely in most schemes.

(*n*) *Formal class hours:* defines that period when students are doing supervised work with a member of staff and includes lectures, seminars, case studies, etc.

(*o*) *Sources of student finance:* an attempt to identify major sources of finance that students at a particular institution tend to draw upon. May identify particular sources unique to an institution.

(*p*) *Student composition 1983/4:* shows class make-up in terms of women and overseas students.

ABBREVIATIONS USED IN COURSE DATA

Masters Degrees

MA	Master of Arts
MBA	Master of Business Administration
MBE	Master of Business Education
MBSc	Master of Busines Science
MEng	Master of Engineering
MHSA	Master of Health Services Administration
MLitt	Master of Literature
MM	Master of Management
MMA	Master of Management and Administration
MMSc	Master of Management Sciences
MPA	Master of Public Administration
MPhil	Master of Philosophy
MPPM	Master of Public and Private Management
MPS	Master of Professional Studies
MSc, MS	Master of Science
MSBA	Master of Science in Business Administration
SM	Master of Science

Doctorates

DBA	Doctor of Business Administration
JD	Jurum Doctor
PhD	Doctor of Philosophy
DPhil	Doctor of Philosophy
DPS	Doctor of Professional Studies

UNIVERSITY OF MELBOURNE
Graduate School of Business Administration, University of Melbourne, Parkville, Victoria 3052, Australia
Tel.: 010 (613) 345 1841

Details: The Graduate School of Business Administration commenced teaching in 1963. Since that date it has awarded the MBA to 750 graduates. There is full college accommodation within the grounds and a large choice of private accommodation available within close proximity.

Admissions Officer: Assistant Registrar.

Courses Offered and Duration: MBA (2 years full-time, but first year may be done part-time over 2 years; 230 enrolments 1984).

Fees: Australian citizens: Nil. Overseas students: Nil. Estimated total annual cost: A$5,000.

Admissions Criteria: Preferred age: 25–35 years. Minimum of 3 years business experience. Any undergraduate degree from a university. Complete fluency in the English language essential.

Business Experience of Current Students: All have a minimum of 3 years.

Specialties: Finance, organisational behaviour, strategy formulation and implementation, quantitative analysis, marketing, industrial relations.

Staff: 17 full-time lecturing staff, and 6 from industrial/commercial organisations.

Teaching Styles Used: Emphasis on case studies.

Assessment: Exam each term plus written and oral assignments.

Class Hours Per Week: 17.

Source of Student Finance: Commonwealth postgraduate awards. BGA loan scheme available.

Student Composition: 15% overseas students, 5% women students.

UNIVERSITY OF NEW SOUTH WALES
Australian Graduate School of Management, University of NSW, PO Box 1, Kensington, Sydney 2033, Australia
Tel.: 010 (612) 663 0351

Details: The School was established by the Australian government as a result of recommendations of a committee of enquiry into Australian postgraduate management education. The first students commenced in 1977. University college accommodation, management library, PDP 11/70 computer. Located 5 miles from Sydney centre and 2 miles from ocean beaches.

Admissions Officer: Assistant Dean.

Courses Offered and Duration: MBA (2 years); MPA (2 years).

Fees: Australian citizens: A$150. Overseas students: A$150. Estimated total annual cost: A$5,000. Australian government requires a fee for student visas (A$2,500).

Admissions Criteria: 3-year degree and 2 years relevant work experience, or 3-year degree and 1 year postgraduate study, or a 4-year degree. GMAT score required.

Specialties: Accounting, finance, economics, organisational behaviour, industrial relations, decision analysis, law, marketing, public policy.

Staff: 20 full-time teaching staff.

Assessment: Varies with instructor but normally continuous assessment.

Source of Student Finance: BGA loan scheme available.

CATHOLIC UNIVERSITY OF LEUVEN
Department of Applied Economic Sciences, Dekenstraat 2, B-3000 Leuven, Belgium

Details: The programme started in 1968 and was opened to executives in 1972. Increasing enrolment of local and international, full-time and part-time students. All facilities associated with a major university are present.

Admissions Officer: Ms. A. Hendrickx.

Placement Officer: Ms A. Hendrickx.

Courses Offered and Duration: MBA – preparatory year (9 months, Class size 30). MBA – full-time programme (12 months, Class size 70). MBA – executive (part-time) programme (42 months, Class size 40).

Fees: Belgian citizens: BFr 12,000. Estimated total annual cost: BFr 180,000.

Admissions Criteria: Business experience of 3 years for executive students. University honours degree in management or economics. GMAT not required but admission test/interview organised by Department may be.

Business Experience of Current Students: 40 executive students with business experience substantially in excess of 3 years.

Specialties: Managerial economics, accountancy, finance, quantitative methods, marketing, international management, organisational behaviour, management information, operations management.

Staff: 15 full-time lecturing staff in school, 3 from other schools teaching on programmes and 3 from industrial/commercial organisations.

Teaching Styles Used: All applied.

Assessment: Coursework (class and examination) and dissertation; examinations twice a year.

Class Hours Per Week: 11.

Source of Student Finance: Own funds or development aid fellowships.

Student Composition: 30% overseas students, 2% women students.

UNIVERSITÉ CATHOLIQUE DE LOUVAIN
Institut d'Administration et de Gestion,
Avenue de l'Espinette 16, B 1348 Louvain-la-Neuve, Belgium

Details: IAG is the Business School of the Université Catholique de Louvain (UCL), now located in the new and growing town of Louvain-la-Neuve, in the French-speaking part of Belgium. Fully equipped university and town (schools, shops, doctors, etc.). Easy train and road connections with Brussels airport. Student and other housing available for short or long periods. Facilities for congresses organised by University Public Relations.

Admissions Officer: Official Belgian Diplomas: Service des Inscriptions, Place de l'Université.
Other diplomas and foreign students: IAG, Mr R. d'Udekem, Directeur, Secretariat Central.

Placement Officer: Amelie Lauve, Placement IAG.

Courses Offered and Duration: Diplôme en Administration des Entreprises (preparatory to MBA, for those with no business background. 9 months minimum, 75 enrolments).
Maîtrise en Administration et en Gestion (equivalent to MBA. 9 months minimum, 35 enrolments).
Maîtrise en Informatique de Gestion (Masters in Data Processing. 9 months minimum, 20 enrolments).
Diplôme Special en Management (9 months minimum, evening seminars, business background required. 80 enrolments 1979).
Diplôme Special d'Economie Appliquée et de Gestion (accent on developing nations. 22 enrolments 1984, for business people from developing nations only).
Doctorat en SEA (equivalent to PhD in Business Administration. 3 years minimum, 10 enrolments).

Fees: BFr 13,500 or BFr 100,000 according to nationality and residence. Estimated total annual cost: BFr 180,000.

Admissions Criteria: 5 years business experience required for both Diplômes Speciaux. University degree required except for DSEAG. Academic and/or business record important.

Specialties: General business policy, data processing, personnel administration, finance, marketing, international business, production management, operation research.

Staff: 45 full-time lecturing staff plus 2 visiting Professors and 2–10 other academics. Several professors are in banking, government or private industry, permanent teaching and research contacts with various organisations.

Teaching Styles Used: Widespread use of case studies and business games; marketing and research surveys; active methods wherever possible; group or individual projects, etc.

Assessment: 3 exam periods (January, June, September), optional repetition of examinations taken. Final paper very important. Individual or group-work basis for over-all appreciation.

Source of Student Finance: Personal resources, scholarships, special agreement between IAG and the Universities of Cornell, Chicago, and Berkeley. Student job service organised in Louvain-la-Neuve.

Student Composition: 32% overseas, 7% women students.

Other Information: Intensive French language course in August; Language Institute has fully equipped laboratories.

McGILL UNIVERSITY
1001 Sherbrooke St. W.,
Montreal, Quebec, Canada, H3A 1G5
Tel.: 0101 (514) 392 4336

Details: The Faculty of Graduate Studies and Research established the Graduate School of Business in 1962, the first class being admitted in the fall of 1963. Merged with undergraduate programme to form Faculty of Management in 1968. Since 1972 the Faculty has been based in downtown Montreal close to the business district. Off-campus housing service is available. Co-ed university hall of residence available. Opportunities to learn sports. Day care facilities for children under 5.

Admissions Officer: Rose Morello.

Placement Officer: Joan Gilday.

Courses Offered and Duration: MBA (2 years, 300 enrolments 1984). PhD (18 months taught, 6 months theory papers, 12 months dissertation).

Fees: Can.$1,140 per year for Canadian citizens; Can$2,100 per year for foreign students. Estimated total annual cost for 1984/5; Can.$10,065 for single students and Can.$11,190+ for married students.

Admissions Criteria: Preferred age: 21+. Previous business experience desirable. Bachelor's degree required. GMAT with a minimum score of 500. Academic and/or professional references required.

Business Experience of Current Students: 2–5 years on average.

Specialties: International business finance, marketing, economics, etc.

Staff: 100 including many from industrial/commercial organisations. Joint MBA/LLB or MBA/BCL programmes available.

Teaching Styles Used: Case studies, business games integrated with traditional lectures.

Assessment: Quizzes, mid-terms, finals, assignments.

Class Hours Per Week: 15.

Source of Student Finance: Management and graduate faculty: Government. BGA loan scheme available.

Student Composition: 50% foreign students, 35% women students.

Other Information: Montreal is a major commercial centre and a cultural centre for French-speaking Canadians.

McMASTER UNIVERSITY
Faculty of Business, McMaster University, Hamilton, Ontario, Canada L8S 4M4
Tel.: 0101 (416) 525 9140

Details: The School of Business was founded in 1964 and became the Faculty of Business in 1968. The School firmly believes in a grounding in theory.

Admissions Officer: R. G. Waterfield, Director of Graduate Admissions.

Placement Officer: Don Bragg.

Courses Offered and Duration: MBA (2 years, 500 enrolments 1984 including part-time).

Fees: Estimated total annual cost: Can$7,275 (tuition and books).

Admissions Criteria: Minimum age of 22 desirable. Business experience of 2–5 years is ideal, although not required. GMAT required. Academic record of mathematics (calculus and linear algebra) and interview also important.

Business Experience of Current Students: 40% with vacational experience; 25% with 1–2 years experience; 25% with 2–5 years experience; 10% with 5 or more years experience.

Specialties: Accounting, finance, international business, market management, marketing research, personnel and human resource management, industrial relations, management information systems, management science, logistics/production/operations.

Staff: 46 teaching staff, of whom 60% engage in external consultancy.

Teaching Styles Used: Class discussion.

Assessment: Informal tests, once a month in year 1, once every 3 months in year 2. Formal examinations once every 3 months throughout. Term projects.

Source of Student Finance: Scholarships, teaching assistantships, some loans available including BGA scheme.

Student Composition: 6% overseas students.

QUEEN'S UNIVERSITY AT KINGSTON
School of Business, Kingston, Ontario, Canada K7L 3N6
Tel.: 0101 (613) 547 5511

Details: In 1919, the School of Commerce of Queen's University at Kingston, Canada, was established with the Department of Political Economy. The School of Business was formed as a separate entity in 1963. Since that time it has offered an Undergraduate

Program in Commerce, a Master's Program in Business Administration and a PhD Program in Management. A residential University for the most part in a small city of 60,000 mid-way between Toronto and Montreal.

Admissions Officer: Donna Lounsbury, Graduate Admissions Officer, MBA Program.

Placement Officer: Donna Lounsbury (Administrative Assistant and Lecturer).

Courses Offered and Duration: BCom (4 academic years).
MBA (2 academic years, 240 enrolments 1984).
PhD in Management Studies (normally 3 years to Degree).

Fees: Canadian citizens: appox. Can.$1,175 (MBA). Overseas students' approx. Can.$6,032 (MBA).

Admissions Criteria: Preferred age: 22–26. Preference for 2 or 3 years' business experience and 4 years' honours undergraduate program, A or High B (or equivalent) academic standing. GMAT required with a score of 560 (preferred minimum). TOEFL required for foreign students.

Business Experience of Current Students: Includes marketing, production, finance, organisation, civil service, consulting, computer services.

Specialties: Marketing, finance, accounting, personnel/behaviour.

Staff: 55 full-time lecturing staff in school, 1–3 per year from other schools teaching on programmes. Consulting work with manufacturing industry, marketing firms, government agencies, etc. Visiting lecturers from business, government, labour and academic institutions. An Executive-In-Residence each year for 4–6 weeks.

Teaching Styles Used: All styles – lectures, seminars, simulation and case studies.

Assessment: 1st year MBA: projects, papers, and examinations at end of each term (65% on 12 course minimum). 2nd year MBA: 2 required and 9 electives (minimum of 65%, 11 courses). Participation projects, papers, seminars; rarely any formal examinations.

Class Hours Per Week: 18 (2 lecture sessions per course; no lectures on Wednesdays).

Student Composition: 2–3% overseas students, 27% women students.

Other Information: Modern management simulation laboratory, master computer with in-house terminals, industrial relations centre on campus.

UNIVERSITY OF WESTERN ONTARIO
School of Business Administration, The University of Western Ontario, London, Canada, N6A 3K7
Tel.: 0101 (519) 679 2111

Details: The School's central focus is an MBA Programme that has a managerial, problem-solving orientation. It is pragmatic and action oriented with a solid theoretical base. The perspective is that of a generalist with special concern for international business, new product and new process technology, and the political environment of business. The school maintains an active contact with the business community through research and casewriting, programmes for experienced managers, guest lectures and alumni affairs.

Admissions Officer: Daphne Stevens, Administrative Assistant – Admissions.

Placement Officer: Mrs Margaret Park.

Courses Offered and Duration: MBA Programme, full-time only (September to April for 2 years, 250 students in each of 2 years). (The School also offers a PhD Programme.)

Fees: Canadian citizens: Can.$1,500 per year. Non-Canadians: Can.$4,500 per year. Estimated total annual cost: Can.$7,000 plus fees.

Admissions Criteria: Undergraduate degree in any discipline with high standing; significant achievement in some activity; full-time work experience preferred; GMAT; TOEFL if necessary. Degree requirement may be waived for mature individuals with outstanding experience or capacity.

Business Experience of Current Students: 80% have at least one year of full-time work experience; average 3–5 years.

Staff: Teaching faculty of 60 full-time; more than 85% have a doctorate from leading North American and European universities.

Teaching Style Used: Learning process based on participation of students in classroom discussion. Over half of class time devoted to case studies; balance – computer simulation, research projects, field trips, audio-visual, negotiations, lectures.

Assessment: Frequent tests, reports, class participation assessments.

Class Hours Per Week: $22\frac{1}{2}$. Estimated time for tests, studies and classes: minimum 60 hours per week.

Source of Student Finance: Scholarships from the School are available. Some student assistantships during second year.

Student Composition: From across Canada and US plus 10% overseas students, 20% women students. Age range 22–40 (average 26).

**FACULTY OF ADMINISTRATIVE STUDIES
YORK UNIVERSITY
4700 Keele St., Toronto, Ontario, Canada, M3J 1P3
Tel.: 0101 (416) 667 2100**

Details: Based in Metropolitan Toronto, the Faculty was founded in 1965 and accepted its first students in 1966. An exchange arrangement operates with Laval University in Quebec City.

Admissions Officer: Carol Pattenden.

Placement Officer: Catherine McPhun-Beatty.

Courses Offered and Duration: MBA (2 years, 900 enrolments 1984).
MPA (50 enrolments 1984).
PhD in Business Administration (20 enrolments 1984).

Fees: Canadian citizens: Can.$129 per course. Foreign students:

Can.$540 per course. Estimated total annual cost for 1984/5: Can.$6,500.

Admissions Criteria: Preferred age 24–27. Previous business experience not required. Bachelor's degree/2nd class standing necessary. GMAT required with a score of 530.

Business Experience of Current Students: 2–3 years.

Specialties: Finance, international business, art administration, organisational behaviour, industrial relations, marketing, managerial economics, MIS, entrepreneurial studies, management accounting, public administration.

Staff: 70.

Teaching Styles Used: Varied methods.

Assessment: Each course graded. Overall grade point average of at least 4.0 required after 14 courses.

Source of Student Finance: Bursaries, loans, scholarships. BGA loan scheme available.

Student Composition: 15% foreign students, 25% women students.

Other Information: Joint MBA/LLB programme available.

INSEAD – EUROPEAN INSTITUTE OF BUSINESS ADMINISTRATION
Boulevard de Constance,
F–77305 Fontainebleau Cedex, France
Tel.: 010 (336) 422 4827

Details: INSEAD, the European Institute of Business Administration, was founded in 1958 as a specifically European business school.

Admissions Officer: Claire Pike.

Placement Officer: Hans Werner.

Courses Offered and Duration: MBA (12 months, Enrolments 140 September, 140 January).

Fees: Estimated total annual cost: Fr60,000 (78/79). Companies pay Fr64,000 (78/79) for sponsored students.

Admissions Criteria: Preferred age 24–31. Two to three years business experience necessary. University degree or professional qualifications and GMAT required. Must have fulfilled all military obligations. Must be fluent in English, French and German.

Business Experience of Current Students: 59% with 4 years or more, 17% with 2–3 years, and 24% with one year or less.

Specialties: 25 electives available.

Staff: 46 plus affiliate, visiting and other professors.

Teaching Styles: Varied with emphasis upon participative learning. Some 350 to 400 cases are studied during the programme.

Assessment: Continuous assessment.

Class Hours Per Week: 90.

Source of Student Finance: Scholarships for women students, and bank and INSEAD loans available. BGA loan scheme available.

Student Composition: 66% foreign students; 8% women students.

Other Information: 100 rooms available in the INSEAD residences.

UNIVERSITY OF CAPE TOWN
The Graduate School of Business, University of Cape Town, Private Bag, Rondebosch 7700, Cape Town, South Africa

Details: The University campus is located near Cape Town on Cecil Rhodes Estate, Groote Schuur. Its situation on the slopes of Devils Peak overlooking the Cape Peninsula is one of the loveliest in the world. The Graduate School of Business was founded in 1965 to provide advanced training in business education leading to a Master of Business Administration degree or an Advanced Diploma in Business Administration. Single accommodation is provided and the School has its own dining hall. The sporting and cultural amenities of the University are available to students of the GSB, and Cape Town is a quarter of an hour away by public transport. The 2 year part-time MBA programme was introduced in 1980. The School runs 18 executive programmes.

Admissions Officer: Dr. Beattie, Director of Admissions and Placement.

Placement Officer: Dr. Beattie.

Courses Offered and Duration: MBA/ADipBA (full-time over 1 year, approx. 70 enrolments 1984); (part-time over 2 years, 40 enrolments 1980).

Fees: Academic: R3,300. Residence: R3,100. Estimated total annual cost: R7,000.

Admissions Criteria: Preferred age 25–35. Normally a Bachelor's or a higher degree required. GMAT required.

Business Experience of Current Students: Recent classes have had on average 5–6 years business experience. Average 30 years.

Specialties: Several courses of particular relevance to South Africa.

Staff: 22 full-time lecturing staff in school, 10 from other schools teaching on programmes and 25 from industrial/commercial organisations. 50 visiting academic staff have attended the school over the past few years.

Teaching Styles Used: The School emphasises participation by members. Extensive use is made of case studies.

Assessment: A mid-term and final examination is set for each course offered during a term. Members are also assessed on participation in class discussions and on written assignments. A research report (technical report) must be completed prior to the end of the academic year.

Class Hours Per Week: 24 minimum.

Source of Student Finance: Bank loans (for SA residents), study grants, bursaries. BGA loan scheme available.

Student Composition: 25–30% overseas students, 5–10% women students.

Other Information: A limited number of non-degree candidates with suitable professional qualifications or extensive business experience are accepted for the MBA programme each year. Such candidates receive the Advanced Diploma in Business Administration. There is an exchange programme with Harvard, Columbia and Northwestern Universities in the second year.

UNIVERSITY OF WITWATERSRAND
Graduate School of Business Administration,
2 St. Davids Place, Parktown, Johannesburg, South Africa
Tel.: 010 (2711) 7163388

Details: The School was established in 1968 and is based in an old mansion in wooded surroundings a mile from the main university campus.

Admissions Officer: The Director.

Courses Offered and Duration: MBA (2 years); Diploma in Personnel Management (10 months).

Fees: R4,500 for all students.

Admissions Criteria: Preferred age: 24–33 years. Some previous business experience preferred. Bachelors degree or professional qualification required. An interview may also be required.

Staff: Totals 14, plus 6 from other schools teaching on programmes. Visiting overseas academics and local executives participate in course teaching.

Teaching Styles: Lectures, group work and tutorials, research and case studies.

Assessment: Tests throughout programmes. Course grades, examination performance and a dissertation taken into account in final assessment. Dissertation must be based upon a research project.

Source of Student Finance: A limited number of industrial bursaries are available. Loans also available. BGA loan scheme available.

IESE, UNIVERSITY OF NAVARRA
Avenida Pearson 21, Barcelona, Spain
Tel.: 010 (343) 204 4100

Details: Founded in 1958 with help from Harvard Business School professors. MBA since 1964, it is the oldest in Europe to their knowledge. Since 1980, the MBA programme has been taught in English or Spanish in the first year, both languages being used in the second. Barcelona has a proven history of 4,000 years with five different cultures. Campus amenities include a student bar and restaurant and although no housing, there is a housing office. The campus is magnificent.

Admissions Officer: Mr Juan Masia.

Placement Officer: Julio Urgel.

Courses Offered and Duration: MBA (21 months full-time, 90 enrolments 1984).
Doctorate (2 to 4 years, dissertation 1 to 2 years, 17 enrolments 1984).

Fees: MBA 380,000 pesetas for both Spanish citizens and foreign students. Estimated total annual cost 1984/85 720,000 pesetas.

Admissions Criteria: MBA: preferred age 24–38 but no limits. Business experience is preferred but not mandatory. University Bachelor degree required. GMAT required but no precise cut-off score exists. Other criteria: references; quality of previous studies; level of motivation of student; level of tenacity to pursue studies; usefulness of the MBA studies to the candidate's objectives; most important, if feasible, an interview.

Business Experience of Current Students: About 30% have business experience of between 2 and 12 years.

Specialties: Bi-lingual MBA (see details); international orientation centred on Spain as a link between Europe and America; international student body.

Staff: 49 full-time, 3 from other schools and 18 from industrial/commercial organisations. IESE is connected with the business world through its executive programmes; more than 3,000 directors of companies have taken these courses.

Teaching Styles Used: All techniques, but predominently case studies.

Assessment: Oral general exam at the end of the first year; course exams are frequent but left to instructors.

Class Hours Per Week: Approximately 30 including workshops.

Source of Student Finance: So varied, description impossible; for Spanish students loans above all; for foreigners usually scholarships. BGA loan scheme available.

Student Composition: 50% foreign students, 8% women students.

Other Information: Studies start in September of each year; students should be fluent at graduation (or before) in the two commercially most important languages in the world.

IMEDE – MANAGEMENT DEVELOPMENT INSTITUTE
23, Chemin de Bellerive, CH–1007 Lausanne, Switzerland
Tel.: 010 (412) 1267112

Details: The Management Development Institute was established in 1957 as an independent foundation in co-operation with, and under the patronage of, the University of Lausanne. The wide range of educational programmes for management offered by the Institute includes both postgraduate and post-experience courses, all of them specifically designed to help international companies in their efforts to accelerate the development of talented managers into professional career executives. The language of instruction is English. The Institute is non-residential, adjacent to Lake Geneva in the Ouchy district.

Admissions Officer: Mrs. Ursula Reesing, IMEDE, CP 1059, CH–1001 Lausanne.

Placement Officer: Mrs. Janette Andre.

Courses Offered and Duration: MBA (11 months, 69 enrolments 1984). Also several executive development courses.

Fees: Swiss citizens: SFr25,000. Estimated total annual cost SFr48,000/52,000 (includes cost of books, lunch at IMEDE 5 days a week).

Admissions Criteria: Preferred age: 25–35. Two or more years of working experience required. University, polytechnic or equivalent degree, references, GMAT test, high level of motivation all important. Enrolment of about 50 participants from 20–25 different countries.

Business Experience of Current Students: 46% with 2–3 years; 28% with 4–5 years; 26% with 6 years or more.

Staff: Teaching faculty of 25 full-time members (of various nationalities).

Teaching Styles Used: Based on case method and field projects.

Assessment: Continuous assessment on the basis of classroom work, written assignments, examinations and other assigned tasks.

Class Hours Per Week: 25 hours (estimated 45 hours group and individual work).

Source of Student Finance: Students may be company- or self-sponsored, some financial assistance in the form of loans granted by a number of banks in various countries. One scholarship only, covering the full fees for the MBA Programme, is offered by the International IMEDE Alumni Association. Applications must reach the School by 1st December. BGA loan scheme available

IMI – INTERNATIONAL MANAGEMENT INSTITUTE
4, Chemin de Conches, CH–1231 Geneva, Switzerland
Tel.: 010 (412) 2471143

Details: Over a 30 year period IMI has offered a great range of courses to over 10,000 managers from 100 countries. The Centre is located in Geneva.

Admissions Officer: The Admissions Office.

Courses Offered and Duration: MBA (Module I 15 weeks; Module II 20 weeks – total duration 9 months).

Admissions Criteria: Minimum of three years work experience required. Bachelors degree is necessary. The programme is specifically aimed at students interested in working in an international environment.

Specialties: International management.

Staff: 18 plus 10 visiting faculty. The Schools Faculty is drawn from 12 nations and 4 continents.

Teaching Styles: The programme includes study trips to two different countries and a five week management consulting project in the field.

Assessment: The course is intensive and the assessment continuous.

Class Hours Per Week: 90 hours total work typical.

Source of Student Finance: Some scholarships are available for students from developing countries. BGA loan scheme available.

Other Information: Associated with the University of Geneva but is an independent institution with full management and budgetary autonomy.

UNIVERSITY OF ASTON MANAGEMENT CENTRE
Nelson Building, Gosta Green, Birmingham B4
Tel.: (021) 359 3011

Details: Based on over 25 years experience of management education the Centre has since its establishment in 1972 risen to become one of the leading business schools with the largest postgraduate programme in the UK. Its Doctoral Programme was selected in 1980 for special support as a "Centre of Excellence" by the Social Science Research Council. The wide range of courses is designed to meet the requirements of students in a variety of interest groups and with diverse career objectives at all stages in their managerial careers. The Centre is housed in a custom-designed building opened in 1978 which contains, in addition to the usual teaching rooms, advanced closed-circuit television and computing equipment, excellent residential accommodation, bar, lounge and dining facilities. Adjacent to the main University library, near to the Sports Hall and opposite the Students Union and Arts Centre, the Centre is located on the main University campus near to the centre of Britain's second largest city.

Admissions Officers: Academic – Dr. Gloria Lee, Director of Postgraduate Studies.

Administrative – Mrs. Jean Coulthard, Postgraduate Executive Secretary.

Placement Officer: John Bailey, Assistant Careers and Appointments Officer.

Courses Offered and Duration: MBA full-time (12 months, 80 enrolments 1984).
MBA part-time (24–36 months, 120 enrolments 1984).
MBA residential (12 months, 14 enrolments 1984).
MSc in Operational Research (12 months, 10 enrolments 1984).
MSc in Operational Research and Management part-time (24 months, 11 enrolments 1984).
MSc in Personnel Management (15 months, 10 enrolments 1984).
MSc in Public Sector Management full-time (12 months, 22 enrolments 1984).
MSc in Public Sector Management part-time (24 months, 11 enrolments 1984).
MSc in Systems Analysis (12 months, 19 enrolments 1984).
Postgraduate Diploma in Business Administration full-time (9 months, 43 enrolments 1984).
Postgraduate Diploma in Business Administration part-time (18–24 months, 63 enrolments 1984).
Postgraduate Diploma in Business Administration residential (6 months, 4 enrolments 1984).
Postgraduate Diploma in Personnel Management (24 months, 22 enrolments 1984).
Postgraduate Diploma in Public Sector Management (24 months, 8 enrolments 1984).
Also offered: Pre-postgraduate Course for overseas students (3–6 months, 26 enrolments 1984). The aim of this course is to prepare overseas students for one-year intensive postgraduate courses in management studies and related areas. It is designed to provide an opportunity to acclimatise to British culture and educational methods while at the same time improving written and spoken English.

Fees: EEC citizens: £1,569 plus Guild fee. Non-EEC citizens: £3,499 plus Guild fee. Residential MBA fees: £4,730 (overseas £6,842).

Admissions Criteria: Preferred age 23–38. Business experience varies from course to course. No previous formal study requirements (except from overseas applicants unable to attend for interview). GMAT not required. Personal interview, previous academic record and previous business experience also important.

Business Experience of Current Students: Mean 8 years experience: 10% with less than 1 years experience; 14% with 1–2 years experience; 21% with 3–5 years experience; 28% with 6–10 years experience; 27% with more than 11 years experience.

Specialties: Organisational behaviour, marketing, operations management, public sector management, personnel management, systems analysis.

Staff: 90, plus research staff, full-time. Small number from other schools teaching on programmes. Several from industrial/ commercial organisations. Links with Ecole Supérieure de Commerce de Lyon.

Teaching Styles Used: Case studies, lectures, seminars, workshops, simulations, closed-circuit TV exercises, projects.

Assessment: 70% formal examinations, 30% continuous assessment; project dissertation.

Class Hours Per Week: 10.

Source of Student Finance: Management Centre Scholarships: Aston University Studentships; ESRC and SERC awards; bank loans from Barclays and Lloyds; BGA schemes.

Student Composition: 20% overseas students, 20% women students.

UNIVERSITY OF BATH SCHOOL OF MANAGEMENT
Claverton Down, Bath BA2 7AY
Tel.: (0225) 61244

Details: The School was founded in 1962 as a department of Bristol College of Science and Technology, became a School of the University in 1966 and transferred to Bath in 1975. The integrated campus is newly developed and there is residential accommodation on and off the campus. Excellent amenities for sport, etc. Very extensive research programme. Opportunities for part-time study.

Admissions Officer: J. R. Nicholls, School of Management.

Placement Officer: University Appointments Officer.

Courses Offered and Duration: MSc in Business Administration (12 months full-time; 3 years part-time, 42 enrolments 1984). MSc in Industrial Marketing (12 months, 3 years part-time). MSc in Industrial Relations (12 months, 3 years part-time).

Fees: UK £1,569, overseas £2,950. Full-time courses.

Admissions Criteria: Preferred age: 25–35. Business experience preferred. First degree or professional qualifications plus DMS or equivalent. GMAT required with a minimum score of 500.

Specialties: Corporate policy, industrial marketing, organisational change and development, manpower studies, industrial relations.

Staff: 36 permanent staff with 10 externally supported research workers; 3 from other schools teaching on programmes; 15 from industrial/commercial organisations. Panel of tutors/advisors on corporate policy studies; also visiting part-time lecturers at managing director level.

Teaching Styles Used: Varied, with an extensive use of project work.

Assessment: Formal examinations plus papers and case reports at end of taught course. Project report.

Class Hours Per Week: 15.

Source of Student Finance: ESRC quota (Business Administration, Industrial Relations), pool (Industrial Marketing), MSC bank loans. BGA loan scheme.

Student Composition: 20% overseas students, 15 women students.

QUEEN'S UNIVERSITY OF BELFAST
Department of Business Studies, Belfast, Northern Ireland
Tel.: (0232) 245133

Details: The department is located on the main campus of the University which is situated close to the main business centre of the city. Student residences are in parkland approximately 10 minutes walk from the main building.

Admissions Officer: David Fleming.

Placement Officers: Kim Clifford or Gill Adrain.

Courses Offered and Duration: MBA (2 years full-time, 3 years part-time). Diploma in Business Administration (1 year full-time, 2 years part-time).

Fees: Full-time £1,494, overseas students £2,046, part-time £374 per annum.

Admissions Criteria: Degree, or exceptional professional qualification and experience. GMAT required.

Specialties: Business policy, small business, marketing.

Staff: 13 staff plus research staff.

Teaching Styles: Lectures, syndicates, case studies, project work, role playing exercises, etc.

Assessment: Continuous plus examinations and project work.

Class Hours: MBA 10 per week, Diploma 28 per week.

Sources of Finance: MSC awards, ESRC, some University awards.

UNIVERSITY OF BRADFORD MANAGEMENT CENTRE
Emm Lane, Bradford, West Yorkshire BD9 4JL
Tel.: (0274) 42299

Details: Two miles from city centre.

Admissions Officer: Professor John Lockyer, Director Postgraduate Programme.

Courses Offered and Duration: MBA – one year, 3 years part-time. 193 enrolments 1984.
PhD programme – minimum of two years full-time.
MPhil by Research – minimum of one year full-time.
Applied MSc by Industrial Project.

Fees: UK citizens: £1,569. Overseas students: £3,150.

Admissions Criteria: Preferred age 21–50, business experience required depends on course. Degree or equivalent.

Business Experience of Current Students: Considerable on MBA courses.

Staff: 55 including 6 professors.

Teaching Styles Used: Case studies, business games, videos, etc.

Assessment: Examinations.

Class Hours Per Week: 9 to 5 daily.

Source of Student Finance: Varied, including ESRC studentships, MSC awards, industrial scholarships, bank loans, BGA loan scheme.

Student Composition: 25% overseas students, 15% women students.

CITY UNIVERSITY BUSINESS SCHOOL
Frobisher Crescent, Barbican Centre, London EC2Y 8HB
Tel.: (01) 920 0111

Details: The Graduate Business Centre of the City University was established in 1966. In 1976 it was redesignated as a Business School on the introduction of a new BSc in Business Studies. In 1982 the School moved to its new location in the Barbican Centre. Amenities include a library, computing facilities, placement service, sports centre 3 minutes away for all kinds of sport, swimming pool within 10 minutes, two large halls of residence, and one block of self-contained flats, Students Union, coffee bar.

Admissions Officer: Dr. Tom Peyton, Director Postgraduate Programmes.

Placement Officer: Mr Gordon Wright in co-operation with Mr Peter Pierce Price, University Careers Advisor.

Courses Offered and Duration: MBA courses (12 months, 3 years part-time) in: Export Management and International Business;

Finance; Industrial Relations and Personnel Management; Management Sciences; Marketing. Enrolments total 220 students. MSc in Business Systems Analysis and Design (12 months). Diploma in Systems Analysis (9 months).

Fees: UK citizens: £1,494. Overseas students: £2,900.

Admissions Criteria: Preferred age: 25–35. 2–5 years business experience preferred. Good honours degree or equivalent qualifications. Personality and motivation, as assessed at interview. GMAT required with a minimum score of 500.

Business Experience of Current Students: 15% with little or no working experience; 20% with under 5 years experience; 30% with 5–10 years experience; 35% with over 10 years experience.

Specialties: Finance, industrial relations and personnel, business strategy, marketing.

Staff: 32 full-time, 6 visiting professors, 11 visiting fellows and Consultant Lecturers. City Advisory Panel with members from all major City of London institutions. Industrial Advisory Panel, with members from a representative range of industrial organisations in private and public sectors.

Teaching Styles Used: Lectures, seminars, tutorials, case studies, exercises, business games, group projects, etc.

Assessment: Written papers in major subjects and in General Management, taken in July; project, completed in August and September; assessed course work in all subjects.

Class Hours Per Week: 12.

Source of Student Finance: ESRC, MSC, university awards, sponsorship. BGA loan scheme.

Student Composition: 30% overseas students, 10% women students.

Other Information: Study and school is particularly directed towards academic and practical preparation for potential senior managers in City and industrial employment.

CRANFIELD INSTITUTE OF TECHNOLOGY
Cranfield School of Management, Cranfield Institute of Technology, Cranfield, Beds. MK43 0AL
Tel.: (0234) 752728

Details: The School of Management is the largest department of the Cranfield Institute of Technology which concentrates on postgraduate post-experience teaching and research in science, technology and management. The Institute, located on a large campus 13 miles south-west of Bedford close to the new city of Milton Keynes, was established as the College of Aeronautics in 1946 and received its Charter as a university in 1969. The first one-year course in business was run at Cranfield in 1963, and the present style of the twelve-month four-term MBA programme was established in 1972. The School's development plan culminated in 1976 with an entirely new building designed to cater for up to 200 MBA students. Single and married student accommodation is available on campus. There are the usual social amenities and facilities for most indoor and outdoor sports, including gliding and sailing.

Admissions Officer: Mr. J. Mapes, Chairman of Admissions Board.

Placement Officer: Mr T. Gore.

Courses Offered and Duration: MBA (12 months, 150 enrolments 1984). Executive MBA (2 years part-time).

Fees: UK citizens: £1,569 approx. Overseas students: £5,250. Hall accommodation: £1,400 approx.

Admissions Criteria: Preferred age: 26–33; 3 years minimum business experience required. Good degree or professional qualifications. GMAT required with a minimum score of 550 for overseas applicants. UK applicants required to satisfy board of admissions on comparable tests and interview on campus.

Business Experience of Current Students: Average business experience of current students is 9 years.

Specialties: Practical approach to business teaching on intensive one-year programme of four eleven-week terms.

Staff: 50 (including 8 professors), 8 from other schools teaching on programmes and about 20 visiting staff from industry and other teaching institutions contribute to specialist options throughout the year.

Teaching Styles Used: Case studies, lectures, exercises/projects, business games, role-playing, etc.

Assessment: Termly examinations and other forms of assessment including class participation.

Class Hours Per Week: 20.

Source of Student Finance: MSC, ESRC, Institute bursaries, sponsorhips, BGA loan scheme.

Student Composition: 20% overseas students, 8% women students.

DURHAM UNIVERSITY BUSINESS SCHOOL
Mill Hill Lane, Durham DH1 3LB
Tel.: (0385) 41919

Details: Durham University Business School started in 1960 as a Business Research Unit concerned mainly with economic and social research in the North East. Expansion of interests led to its first teaching course for managers in 1965, and in 1967 the MSc programme was launched. Working links with industry have been strong since inception, and industry has supplied a significant proportion of the funds for the new purpose-built Business School building which opened in October 1977. Full teaching and library facilities on site. Accommodation in colleges or in non-college accommodation through the Graduate Society.

Admissions Officer: Mr Robin Smith.

Courses Offered and Duration: MSc in Management Studies (12 months, 34 enrolments 1984; 2 year part-time, 14 enrolments 1984).

Fees: UK citizens: £1,500. Overseas students: £3,500. Estimated total annual cost £4,000—5,000.

Admissions Criteria: Preferred age: 25–40, but places available for suitable immediate graduates. 3 years working experience desirable, not necessarily confined to private sector. Good honours degree or equivalent professional qualifications and experience. GMAT required. Application form, references and interview also important.

Business Experience of Current Students: Average 4 years in accountancy, engineering, hotel management, banking, pharmacy.

Specialties: Human resource management, export marketing, small business management and management of the arts.

Staff: 15 staff in school, plus several from industrial organisations.

Teaching Styles Used: Lectures, case studies, small group work, projects.

Assessment: Written examinations January and May, dissertation following project period.

Class Hours Per Week: 16.

Source of Student Finance: ESRC quota awards, MSC, BGA loans. Some students are sponsored by their employers.

Student Composition: 40% overseas students, 15% women students.

Other Information: The School has a large and successful Post-experience Programme through which teaching staff have continuing links with industry. In addition, the School has developed, in the Small Business Centre, a Centre of excellence.

UNIVERSITY OF EDINBURGH
Scottish Business School, University of Edinburgh Division, Department of Business Studies, William Robertson Building, 50 George Square, Edinburgh EH8 9JY
Tel.: (031) 667 1011

Details: The Department, one of the oldest in the UK, is located near the centre of the capital city of Scotland. The University of Edinburgh has excellent teaching and student facilities and is considered one of the major British universities.

Admissions Officer: Dr. John Henley, Course Director.

Placement Officer: L.A. Bassett, Careers Advisor.

Courses Offered and Duration: MBA Full-time (12 months, 45 enrolments 1984).
MBA Part-time (3 years, 33 enrolments 1984).
MPhil Full-time (12 months).
Dip.BA Full-time (9 months).

Fees: UK £1,500, overseas approx. £3,000.

Admissions Criteria: Preferred age: 23+. Business experience preferred but not necessary if academically well qualified and evidence available (vacation work, non-academic university activities) that the participant is enthusiastic, energetic and mature for his/her age. A good honours degree or equivalent, and the GMAT together with sound references are required. Where feasible students are interviewed.

Business Experience of Current Students: Majority have more than 2 years business experience.

Staff: 25.

Teaching Styles Used: A variety of systems as appropriate to the subject matter.

Assessment: 5 final examinations in June. Potential MBA candidates must achieve 60% or better to continue to the preparation and presentation of an approved MBA dissertation in September.

Source of Student Finance: Various: SED for Scottish supported students; also Manpower Service Awards.

Student Composition: 25% overseas students, 20% women students.

UNIVERSITY OF GLASGOW
Division of the Scottish Business School, The University, Glasgow
Tel.: (041) 339 8855

Details: The School has been in existence since 1953. The early activities centred on non-graduating post-experience work which has now evolved into a mainly graduate programme. In particular, the

University of Glasgow has pioneered the development of the part-time MBA programme which is now attended by over 120 managers working in organisations in Scotland.

Admissions Officer: Professor David Weir.

Placement Officer: Mr J.D. Logan, Appointments Office, University of Glasgow.

Courses Offered and Duration: MBA (3 years part-time, 111 enrolments 1984).
MEng in Engineering Management (3 years part-time, 30 enrolments 1984).
PhD/MLitt (3 years, 11 enrolments 1984).

Admissions Criteria: Any age PhD/MLitt. Preferred age 30–45 MBA/MEng. Business experience: normally at least 5 years for MBA, 2 years for MEng. Academic requirements: degree or equivalent for MBA/MEng, plus evidence of actual and potential progress.

Business Experience of Current Students: Very extensive. From 5 years Junior Managerial/Technical to 20 years, now at Director Level.

Specialties: General management and business policy; production management; organisational behaviour; industrial relations; limited specialisms in finance and marketing.

Staff: 15 full-time, 3 part-time, 3 from other schools teaching on programmes.

Teaching Styles Used: All forms of teaching are used. Staff are strongly encouraged to use non-traditional methods wherever appropriate.

Assessment: Regular assignments and annual examinations for MEng and MBA. Dissertation/thesis for MLitt/PhD.

Class Hours Per Week: 4–5.

Source of Student Finance: Employers, self.

HENLEY – THE MANAGEMENT COLLEGE
Greenlands, Henley-on-Thames, Oxon. RG9 3AU
Tel.: (0491) 66454

Details: Europe's "senior" business school, founded in 1946 and offering its first course in 1948, the college is an independent organisation without political, social or economic bias. It is ideally situated on the banks of the Thames, about two miles from the town of Henley. Its function is the education of managers for further responsibilities so that they will run efficient, effective and profitable enterprises. It has close associations with Brunel University for the purposes of study for higher degrees.

Admissions Officer: Professor David Birchall.

Courses Offered and Duration: MBA Full-time (45 enrolments 1984). A two-year sandwich course leading to an MBA degree. This involves 28 weeks of residential study at Henley and 39 weeks of practical project work in organisations. A further period of 26 weeks on a dissertation leads to the MBA degree. The philosophy of the programme is based on individual development with extensive use of the tutorial methods. It is designed, primarily, for men and women with managerial experience.

The MSc part-time and distance learning Postgraduate Management Studies Programme. This complements the Masters Programme, and involves a minimum of two years' part-time study. It is designed for those who cannot obtain sufficient leave to pursue the full-time course. (72 enrolments 1984).

The Research Programme, established in conjunction with postgraduates' studies, and involving individually based research for a higher degree at both MPhil and PhD level.

Other courses include post-experience courses for managers who have substantial experience, and short (one week) courses on specialised topics. The Management Development and Advisory Service provides specialist services on an in-company basis, particularly for senior and middle management in terms of development and problem solving.

Fees: MBA £4,500 (overseas £5,625), MSc £420 part-time, MSc distance learning £1,000. MPhil/PhD £1,930 (overseas £3,630).

Admissions Criteria: Entrants normally sponsored by their own organisations. Minimum of two or three years substantive experience in industry, commerce or other organisations normally required.

Staff: Drawn both from Henley and from Brunel University, Henley has an academic staff of 35 plus 24 visiting fellows.

Teaching Styles Used: Learning by working on tasks and in small groups. Participants are encouraged to "manage" their own learning, each student being supervised by a Programme Tutor.

Assessment: Continuous assessment is used which includes written reports on "in-service" work and conventional examination. The submission of a dissertation is required for the award of the MBA degree.

Other Information: A special feature of the Henley/Brunel MBA programme is the opportunity to work on a substantial project within a sponsoring/nominating organisation during three 14 week "in-service" periods.

UNIVERSITY OF HULL
Department of Management Systems and Sciences
Hull HU6X 7RX
Tel.: (0482) 46311

Details: The department is on the main campus of the University about 2 miles from the city centre.

Admissions Officer: Michael Jackson.

Courses Offered: MA in Management Systems (12 months full-time, 3 years part-time).
MSc in Management Sciences (12 months full-time, 3 years part-time).

Fees: £1,718 full-time, overseas £3,480 full-time.

Admissions Criteria: A good degree is required. Business experience preferred.

Specialties: Microcomputer applications, systems theory, organisation development.

Teaching Styles: Lectures, seminars, project work in organisations.

Staff: The department has 9 full-time staff.

Sources of Finance: University awards, MSC, BGA loans scheme.

UNIVERSITY OF LANCASTER
Gillow House, Bailrigg, Lancaster LA1 4YX
Tel.: (0524) 65201

Details: The School of Management and Organisation Sciences consists of a federation of departments each of which has developed a considerable reputation within its specialisation. The school was established in 1969 to promote the interests of its constituent departments which were established between 1964 and 1968. Departments of the School are housed on the campus which is three miles south of Lancaster and which overlooks Morecambe Bay and the Lake District.

Admissions Officer: Dr. A. Hindle, School of Management and Organisational Sciences.

Courses Offered and Duration: MA in Accounting and Finance (12 months).
MA in Business Analysis (12 months) — interdepartmental course.
MA in Marketing (12 months).
MSc in Operational Research (12 months).
MA in Organisational Psychology (12 months).
MA in Systems in Management (12 months).
Diploma in Operational Research (9 months).
MA in Management Learning (24 months, part-time).
Diploma in Business Analysis (9 months).
Total Masters student intake for 1984 was 147.

Fees: UK citizens: £1,480. Overseas students: £3,300. Estimated total cost: £4,000–6,000.

Admissions Criteria: No preferred age. Several years' working experience preferred for most courses. Good honours degree or equivalent professional qualification. Experienced applicants with non-standard qualifications are considered on their merits. The GMAT and other tests are used as selection aids and applicants are interviewed wherever possible. Operational Research requires a good honours degree normally in a subject with considerable quantitative content, and Organisational Psychology normally requires a good honours degree with high psychology or social science content, but in each case the diploma course offers a route for those wishing to transfer from other disciplines.

Business Experience of Current Students: 21% with vacation experience only; 26% with 1–2 years experience; 18% 3–5 years experience; 35% with 5 years or more experience.

Specialties: Each department is an established leader in its own field.

Staff: 79 senior staff with a further 35 in its associated departments.

Teaching Styles Used: Varied. Emphasis is laid on the inclusion of a meaningful practical project which often involves participation in a major on-going consultancy or research activity. (The School has associated with it three consulting companies.)

Assessment: Assessment criteria vary from department to department but generally include a dissertation on the project (consultancy or library based), open and closed book examinations, major case exercises and other set tasks and assignments.

Source of Student Finance: ESCR, SERC, FME bursaries, MSC and BGA loan schemes.

UNIVERSITY OF LEEDS
Department of Management Studies, Leeds LS2 9JT
Tel.: (0532) 31751

Details: The department is located on the main campus of the University about one mile from the city centre.

Admissions Officer: Dr. John Haynes.

Courses Offered and Duration: MBA (12 months full-time, 35 enrolments 1984).

Fees: Approximately £5,000. (The course is primarily for mature overseas students.)

Admissions Criteria: Normally mature mid-career graduates working in developing countries who are sponsored by their companies.

Business Experience: Minimum of 4 years, average of 14 years. Average age is 38.

Specialties: Project management linked with company requirements.

Staff: 15 full-time and other part-time staff.

Assessment: Examination and coursework. There is a final dissertation based on company work.

Class Hours: 17 overall but higher during the first 4 weeks.

Finance: All students are company sponsored.

LONDON GRADUATE SCHOOL OF BUSINESS STUDIES
Sussex Place, Regent's Park, London NW1 4SA
Tel.: (01) 262 5050

Details: The London Business School was founded in 1965 as a result of the Franks Report. In 1970 it moved into its current premises at a Nash Terrace in Regent's Park and has substantial residential accommodation for students and managers on executives programmes.

Admissions Officer: Prof. Julian Franks, Director of MSc Programme.

Placement Officer: Ms. A. Jackson.

Courses Offered and Duration: MSc in Business Studies (21 months, 3 years part-time).
PhD Programme ($2\frac{1}{2}$–3 years).
London Sloan Fellowship Programme (9 months).

Fees: MSc/PhD: Home students: £1,494 (1984). Overseas students: £3,650 (1984). London Sloan Fellowship Programme: £7,300 (1984). MSc part-time £1,037. Overseas students: £2,433.

Admissions Criteria: For MSc mixed, based upon degree performance, a detailed application form, personal references and the results of the GMAT. 2–5 years business experience ideal though less accepted in special cases. Applicants will normally be interviewed by a Faculty member and an alumnus.
For the London Sloan Fellowship Programme no previous qualifications are required.

UK

Business Experience of Current Students: Average age 27 on entry.

Staff: About 100 professional management teachers and researchers.

Teaching Styles Used: For MSc varied depending upon course material. There is an emphasis on learning in groups and students are required to undertake substantial long vacation and second year projects.

Assessment: For MSc each student is given a grade on individual courses throughout the programme. The award of the MSc is based on a final written examination at the end of the second year, together with an overall assessment of the grades achieved during the two years of the programme.

Source of Student Finance: ESRC studentships and Department of Education bursaries. BGA loan scheme.

Student Composition: Increasingly international.

Other Information: The London Business School initiated, together with HEC Paris and New York University, an International Management Programme allowing 10 MSc students to spend their second year at two overseas business schools. Bilateral exchanges of second year students also takes place with Chicago, Wharton, Harvard, Western Ontario and other schools.

LONDON SCHOOL OF ECONOMICS
Houghton Street, London WC2A 2AE
Tel.: (01) 405 7686

Details: The London School of Economics has its own building on Houghton Street by The Aldwych in the centre of London.

Admissions Officer: Dr. I. Stephenson, Co-ordinator, Graduate School.

Courses Offered and Duration: MSc in Business (2 years full-time, 3 years part-time, 276 enrolments 1984).
Diploma in Business Studies (1 year full-time, 2 years part-time).

Fees: UK and EEC students £1,494. Other overseas students £3,650.

Admissions Criteria: Good Honours degree. Preferred age 21–35. Business experience preferred.

Specialties: Industrial relations, personnel management, economic models for business systems.

Staff: 40 academic staff in the School.

Teaching Styles Used: Lectures, syndicates, case studies, project work.

Sources of Finance: ESRC, MSC, some University awards, BGA loan scheme.

UNIVERSITY OF LONDON, IMPERIAL COLLEGE
Management Science Dept., London SW7 2BX
Tel.: (01) 589 5111

Details: Work in the Management Science Field at Imperial College started in 1955. The college is situated in South Kensington not far from the Albert Hall. It has some of Britain's best university facilities and students make considerable use of these.

Admissions Officer: Dr. J.O. Jenkins.

Placement Officer: A.J. Lodge.

Courses Offered and Duration: MSc in Management Science (12 months, 75 enrolments in 1984).

Fees: UK and EEC students: £1,494 (1984). Other overseas students: £5,000 (1984). These fees are subject to alteration for 1985.

Admissions Criteria: Preferred age 21–35. 1–5 years business experience preferred. First or second class honours degree. GMAT required with a minimum score of 85%. Personal interview, referees' reports, academic record also important.

Business Experience of Current Students: 16% with 1–2 years experience; 5% with 3–4 years experience; 22% with 5 or more years experience.

Specialties: Operational research, production and operations, management finance, quantitative methods, computing and simulation.

Staff: 21 full-time academic staff; visiting lecturers from the LSE; visiting lecturers from National Westminster Bank; Engineering Employers Federation, British Oxygen; McLintock, Mann, Lafrentz.

Teaching Styles Used: Lectures, seminars, case studies, research projects, business games, company visits.

Assessment: Formal examinations, continuous assessment of course-work and project report. Formal examinations consist of five papers taken at the end of the course.

Class Hours Per Week: 17.

Source of Student Finance: SERC awards, BTR Ltd and Ford of Europe Inc bursaries, college bursaries, University of London postgraduate studentships, MSC awards, bank loans under the student bank loan scheme. BGA loan scheme.

Student Composition: 44% overseas students, 30% women students.

Other Information: The MSc programme comprises 11 compulsory core subjects and an elective choice from a further 45 course subjects. There is, therefore, great flexibility in the available choice, which makes it possible for the individual student to tailor the programme to meet his or her special needs. Recommended groupings of electives are provided in the form of four modules: production and operations management, business management, operations research, finance.

LOUGHBOROUGH UNIVERSITY OF TECHNOLOGY
Department of Management Studies
Loughborough, Leicestershire LE11 3TU
Tel.: (0509) 263171

Details: The department is on the main campus which is located approximately one mile from the city centre.

Admissions Officer: Dr. M. King.

Courses Offered and Duration: MSc in Management Studies (3 years part-time).

Fees: Approximately £300 p.a.

Admissions Criteria: Degree or equivalent professional qualification. Previous business experience is a requirement.

Specialties: Small firms, personnel systems, microprocessor applications, marketing.

Teaching Styles Used: Lectures, case studies, role playing exercises.

Class Hours: 6 hours per week plus project work and exercises.

Assessment: Examinations each year plus reports and dissertation project in the third year.

UNIVERSITY OF MANCHESTER
**Manchester Business School, University of Manchester,
Booth Street West, Manchester M15 6PB
Tel.: (061) 273 8228**

Details: Manchester Business School was established in 1965 as a result of the Franks and Normanbrook Reports. It has developed a distinctive approach to teaching which departs from the traditional groupings of subject matter and seeks to develop basic skills and analytical abilities which will be applicable to any kind of management problem. There is a wide range of lecture and seminar rooms, 154 study bedrooms (each with its own shower/bathroom) and excellent library and computing facilities. The new building on the university campus is well within walking distance of the city centre.

Admissions Officer: Mrs. Barbara Kennerley.

Placement Officer: Mr Colin Laycock.

Courses Offered and Duration: MBA (18 months full-time, 80 enrolments, 3 years part-time, 40 enrolments 1984).
Dip BA (9 months full-time, 2 years part-time).

Fees: UK citizens £1,494 p.a. Overseas students £3,700 p.a.

Admissions Criteria: Preferred age 24–30, 3–5 years business experience preferred. First degree or approved professional qualification. GMAT required with variable score. Previous academic record, personal interview, and business experience are all taken into account. Selection conferences are held.

Business Experience of Current Students: Ranges from 0–16 years. Average 3 years.

Specialties: Group work on live projects within different organisations, joint development activities, international centre for banking and finance, new enterprise group.

Staff: 35 staff. Speakers are invited as appropriate. Visiting speakers on courses, co-operation in course projects, post-experience courses and joint development activities.

Teaching Styles Used: Lectures, seminars, case studies, business games, field projects and workshops.

Assessment: Project performance, case studies and essays during the course, formal examinations at the end of first year.

Class Hours Per Week: 20–22.

Source of Student Finance: ESRC awards, Business School bursaries, scholarships, and company sponsorships. BGA loan scheme.

Student Composition: 22% overseas students, 21% women students.

UNIVERSITY OF MANCHESTER INSTITUTE OF SCIENCE AND TECHOLOGY
Department of Management Sciences, UMIST, PO Box 88, Sackville Street, Manchester M60 1QD
Tel: (061) 236 3311

Details: University of Manchester Institute of Science and Technology is 10 minutes walk from the city centre, Piccadilly Station and University campus centre. In 1918, the Department of Industrial Administration was founded and in 1965, the Department of Management Sciences. UMIST celebrated its 150th anniversary in 1974. Halls of Residence and Accommodation Office are shared with Manchester University as are the extensive library, games and Student Union facilities. Manchester is a major cultural, industrial, etc. centre.

Admissions Officer: Postgraduate Admissions Officer.

Placement Officer: Mr B. Holloway, Careers and Appointments Service, University of Manchester, Manchester 13.

Courses Offered and Duration: MSc in Management Sciences (12 months full-time, 48 enrolments 1984; 3 years part-time, 123 enrolments 1984).
MSc in Marketing (12 months full-time, 10 enrolments).
MSc in Organisational Psychology (12 months full-time).

Fees: UK citizens: £1,569. Overseas students £3,150.

Admissions Criteria: Business experience required varies from course to course. First degree is normally required. GMAT required with a score of 500 for overseas applicants. Qualifications equivalent to honours degrees will also be considered.

Business Experience of Current Students: Most students have had employment experience other than vacation work. Experience includes public sector.

Specialties: International business, finance and control, production, personnel management.

Staff: 50 staff including 6 professors.

Teaching Styles Used: Full range of teaching styles employed.

Assessment: Assessment based on examination at end of taught period and dissertation submitted at the end of course.

Class Hours Per Week: 14.

Source of Student Finance: ESRC awards, industrial studentships from covenanted funds, MSC awards. BGA loan scheme.

Student Composition: 43% overseas students, 17% women students.

Other Information: Research degrees, MSc and PhD, are also offered.

UNIVERSITY OF OXFORD, TEMPLETON COLLEGE
Oxford Centre for Management Studies,
Kennington Road, Kennington, Oxford OX1 5NY
Tel.: (0865) 735422

Details: The programme, which started in the late 1960s, is limited to an entry of 10 per year, focusing on small group work and catering for individual needs. Students have the use of Oxford colleges and libraries; accommodation for single and married students; Oxford Management Centre library, common room and dining room. The programme is based at the Oxford Centre for Management Studies.

Admissions Officer: Senior Tutor.

Placement Officer: Oxford University Appointments Committee and Senior Tutor, Oxford Centre for Management Studies.

Courses Offered and Duration: MPhil in Management Studies (21 months, 10 enrolments).
MLitt. in Management Studies (21 months).
MSc in Industrial Relations (21 months).
DPhil in Management Studies (33 months).

Fees: UK citizens: £2,500. Overseas students: £3,900.

Admissions Criteria: Preferred age 21–35. Business experience desirable. First or upper second degree. Good references, high quality written work, suited to Oxford emphasis on individual and small group work also important. GMAT required.

Business Experience of Current Students: 60% have no previous experience other than vacation work. The remainder have varied amounts of experience in general management, law, government, management science, management services, banking and finance.

Specialties: Accounting, economics, industrial relations, management information systems, organisational behaviour.

Staff: 12 staff in Oxford Centre, 6 Associate Fellows and other Lecturers from departments elsewhere in the University. Close contacts also exist with corporate member firms of the Management Centre.

Teaching Styles Used: Tutorials, seminars, lectures, case studies, projects, business games.

Assessment: At end of course two general exams and two selected options, plus thesis.

Class Hours Per Week: 12 in first year.

Source of Student Finance: ESRC awards, bank loans, Rhodes and other scholarships. BGA loan scheme.

Student Composition: 50% overseas students, 20% women students.

Other Information: Students can and do transfer from the MPhil to the MLitt during their course, or at the end of it to the DPhil course. Students mix with managers on post-experience programmes at the Management Centre.

UNIVERSITY OF SALFORD
Department of Business and Administration, Salford M5 4WT
Tel.: (061) 736 5843

Details: The Royal Technical Institute of Salford was founded in 1896 and in 1967 became the University of Salford. The department is on the main campus, a 34 acre site on Peel Park on the boundary of the cities of Salford and Manchester.

Admissions Officer: Margaret Marsden.

Courses Offered: MSc Marketing and a foreign language (2–3 years part-time).
MSc Employment Studies (2–3 years part-time).
Diploma in Employment Studies (18 months part-time).

Fees: £245 per annum.

Admissions Criteria: A good honours degree or an equivalent professional qualification.

Business Experience: All students will be working or have several years of outside experience.

Specialties: Political economy of Europe, marketing information and research, industrial sociology.

Staff: 21 academic staff plus 2 industrial tutors.

Teaching Styles Used: Lectures, seminars, case studies, projects and role playing exercises.

Assessment: Course work, examinations and project dissertation.

Sources of Finance: Company sponsorship, self, BGA loan scheme.

UNIVERSITY OF SHEFFIELD
Division of Economic Studies, Sheffield S10 2TN
Tel.: (0742) 78555

Details: Postgraduate business programmes have been offered at Sheffield since 1961. The present programme is a wide ranging course covering business economics, organisational behaviour and industrial relations, marketing, quantitative analysis, accounting and financial management, and business policy. Teaching takes place in the Crookesmoor Building, which houses the teaching and research library for the Division of Economic Studies, and a fully equipped computer terminals room. The course may be taken part-time.

Admissions Officer: Dr Arthur Meidan, Director Postgraduate Programme.

Placement Officer: Mr D.B. Read, Careers Advisory Service.

Courses Offered and Duration: MBA (1 year full-time, 3 years part-time).
MA in Accounting and Financial Management (1 year full-time, 3 years part-time).
DipBA (full-time and part-time).

Fees: UK citizens £1,494. Overseas students £2,900. Part-time £233.

Admissions Criteria: Second class honours degree or professional qualification; GMAT required for candidates without an upper second. Relevant experience an advantage.

Business Experience of Current Students: Half have three or more years business experience.

Staff: 14 staff members of the Division of Economic Studies teach on the course. There are several visiting lecturers.

Teaching Styles Used: Lectures, tutorials, problem classes, role playing exercises, computer based business games, case study discussions, projects.

Assessment: Assessed course work counts for between 30% and 50% of each course, depending on subject.

Class Hours Per Week: About 15.

Source of Student Finance: ESRC, MSC, bank loans, BGA loan scheme.

Student Composition: 40% overseas students, 10% women students.

UNIVERSITY OF STRATHCLYDE BUSINESS SCHOOL
130 Rottenrow, Glasgow G4 0GE
Tel.: (041) 552 7141

Details: Established in its present form in 1970, the School is an integral department of the University of Strathclyde and also contributes to the programme of the Scottish Business School. Both postgraduate and post-experience students are taught in the one building, with consequent benefit to the exchange of ideas and experiences. All full-time students are members of the Students' Association of the University. Accommodation is not especially difficult to find, and includes a senior Hall of Residence for postgraduate students at Bearsden, some 5 miles from the city centre.

Admissions Officer: Gordon Anderson, MBA Programme Director.

Courses Offered and Duration: MBA full-time (12 months, 47 enrolments 1984).
MBA part-time (36 months, 120 enrolments 1984).
MBA by distance learning (100 enrolments).

Fees: UK citizens: £1,494. Overseas students: £3,450 total. Part-time: £375.

Admissions Criteria: Preferred age: 26–35. Each application is considered on an individual, overall basis. Thus, while candidates who have a degree plus 2 years' minimum experience are preferred, the School will still consider applicants ' who have no formal academic qualifications but an outstanding business record or, conversely, some graduates with less than the minimum experience. GMAT not required but may be requested by selection committee.

Business Experience of Current Students: 5% with 1–2 years experience; 50% with 2–5 years experience; 45% with more than 5 years experience.

Specialties: The individual subject areas of the MBA course are each taught by lecturers from the University's specialist departments. The Business School's particular expertise lies in drawing these various threads together and illustrating their practical applications; this is especially the case in the teaching of Business Policy.

Staff: 19 full-time lecturing staff plus 21 from other schools teaching on programmes, and about 20 from industrial/commercial organisations (number of guest lecturers/speakers varies from year to year – availability is a critical factor).

Teaching Styles Used: All teaching styles from lectures and tutorials to case studies, business games, individual projects and computer exercises.

Assessment: Formal examinations at the end of each term, plus continuous assessment in some subjects and a dissertation.

Class Hours Per Week: 20 full-time, 5 part-time.

Source of Student Finance: ESRC, studentships, Scottish Education Department, university studentships, employer sponsorships (especially for the part-time course). BGA loan scheme.

Student Composition: 33% foreign students.

UNIVERSITY OF WALES INSTITUTE OF SCIENCE AND TECHNOLOGY
2 Museum Place, Cardiff CF1 3BG
Tel.: (0222) 42588

Details: The centre for Graduate Management Studies was founded in 1971. UWIST is situated in parkland in the Civic Centre of Cardiff close to the Welsh Office and the National Museum. The Department is located in the Aberconway building close to the city centre.

Admissions Officer: Mr A.D. Hall, Assistant Registrar.

Placement Officer: Mr D. Mutlow, Director, Joint University Careers and Appointments Service, 53 Park Place, Cardiff.

Courses Offered and Duration: MBA (1 year full-time, 40 enrolments, 3 years part-time).
DipBA (9 months full-time, 19 enrolments, 2 years part-time).

Fees: UK citizens £1,569. Overseas students £3,150.

Admissions Criteria: An honours degree is required. A reasonable level of mathematics and statistics is desirable. Business experience is desirable. Non-graduates with approved professional qualifications may be considered.

Business Experience of Current Students: 17% with 1–2 years experience; 22% with 2–5 years experience; 17% with 5 or more years experience.

Specialties: Operations research; personnel management; finance and accounting; management systems.

Staff: 22 staff plus others drawn from several departments of UWIST. About 60% of those involved in the degree course engage in external consulting.

Assessment: Formal examination and dissertation.

Source of Student Finance: A number of students have in the past been sponsored by the MSC. BGA loan scheme.

Class Hours Per Week: 30 plus.

UNIVERSITY OF WARWICK
School of Industrial and Business Studies,
Coventry, Warwickshire CV4 7AL
Tel.: (0203) 24011

Details: Business courses started in 1966. From the start the University has offered Masters programmes of high quality. Since then its range of activities has broadened to include a substantial undergraduate programme, higher degrees by research and a range of short post-experience programmes as well as the four 12-month taught Masters programmes. The University is on a 450 acre rural site on which about two-thirds of the 4,500 students are accommodated. Besides extensive sporting facilities the University has a magnificent Arts Centre and a Sports Centre with indoor swimming pool, gymnasium, squash-courts and other facilities. The Shakespeare theatre at Stratford-upon-Avon is some 15 miles away.

Admissions Officer: See under Courses Offered and Duration.

Courses Offered and Duration: MBA (12 months, 3 years part-time, 50 enrolments) Professor B.T. Houlden.
MSc in Management Science and Operational Research (12 months, 3 years part-time) Professor R.C. Tomlinson.
MA in Industrial Relations (12 months, 3 years part-time) Professor G.S. Bain.

Fees: UK citizens £1,494 (1984). Overseas students £2,968.

Admissions Criteria: Preferred age 21–35. Business experience of 2–5 years preferred. First or upper second degree or professional equivalent required in most cases. GMAT required in some instances with a score of approximately 550. Most candidates are interviewed for motivation and personality.

Business Experience of Current Students: Average 4 years.

Specialties: The School is organised into six areas of concentration under a professor – industrial relations, financial management, marketing, business policy, organisational behaviour and operational research systems, small business.

Staff: 37 full-time lecturing staff of whom 80% have had full-time experience of business. Four top executives from industry and the public sector are closely associated with the programmes.

Teaching Styles Used: Lectures, case studies, seminars, tutorials, projects.

Assessment: MA Industrial Relations: coursework assessed in June, dissertation assessed in October. MSc courses include piece of assessed work set per subject per term, examinations once a year in June, practical/research project dissertation to be completed during September.

Class Hours Per Week: 10–16.

Source of Student Finance: Company sponsorship, university scholarships, ESRC, SERC, MSC bank loans, BGA loan scheme.

Student Composition: 20% overseas students, 11% women students.

UNIVERSITY OF CALIFORNIA, BERKELEY
Graduate School of Business Administration, University of California, 350 Barrows Hall, Berkeley, California 94720
Tel.: 0101 (415) 642 1405

Details: The Business Programme was started in 1898, the MBA Programme in 1955. Berkeley is the second oldest collegiate school of business in the United States. PhD programmes are also offered. The University is one of the great educational institutions in the world with outstanding library, computer and other support services. The San Francisco Bay area offers access to almost any business environment in addition to unparalleled cultural and recreational activities.

Admissions Officer: Robert L. Bailey, Director of Admissions.

Placement Officer: Career Planning and Placement, Assistant Director, 26 Barrows Hall.

Courses Offered and Duration: More than 100 courses in all aspects of Business and Management (1–2 years depending on background, 550 enrolments 1980).

Fees: Californian residents: $1,620. Non-residents: $6,100.

Admissions Criteria: Business experience of 1–2 years preferred but not required. Recognised bachelor's degree. GMAT required.

Statement of Purpose, letters of reference, other evidence of leadership potential also important.

Business Experience of Current Students: Post-baccalaureate: 36% with 0–1 year; 14% with 1–2 years; 11% with 2–3 years; 12% with 3–4 years; 27% with more than 4 years.

Specialties: Quantitative and analytical techniques emphasised in a framework of the political and social environment.

Staff: 82 full-time, 31 part-time. 5–10 visitors from other schools.

Teaching Styles Used: Wide variety of teaching styles and tools employed; no commitment to any one method. Applied management projects required of all MBA students.

Assessment: Course examinations each quarter; applied management project at end of programme.

Class Hours Per Week: 16.

Source of Student Finance: Scholarships, assistantships, loans and part-time employment; BGA loan scheme available.

Student Composition: 14% overseas students, 34% women students.

Other Information: Students required to select field of emphasis, e.g. accounting, finance, marketing, political and social environment, general management.

UNIVERSITY OF CALIFORNIA, LOS ANGELES
UCLA Graduate School of Management,
405 Hilgard Ave., Los Angeles, California 90024

Details: GSM is a professional school which functions as part of a great university. Its primary mission is to train men and women who aspire to leadership positions in business, government and not for profit organisations. Located in Westwood, 10 minutes from the ocean.

Admissions Officer: Director of Student Affairs and Admissions.

Courses Offered: MBA.

Fees: Californian residents: $1,590. Non-residents and overseas students: $5,828.

Admissions Criteria: Preferred age 24+. 2 years work experience preferred. Calculus required. GMAT required. TOEFL – minimum 580 – only required for students who attended non-English-speaking institutions.

Business Experience of Current Students: 2 years average.

Specialties: 14 areas of concentration; nucleus and field study components of the curriculum.

Staff: 94 in faculty.

Teaching Styles Used: Lecture, case study, experiental learning, team consulting.

Assessment: Normal A,B,C grading. Exams vary by course.

Class Hours Per Week: 16.

Source of Student Finance: Savings, financial aid, part-time jobs.

Student Composition: 15% overseas students, 35% women students.

CARNEGIE-MELLON UNIVERSITY
Schenley Park, Pittsburgh, Pennsylvania
Tel.: 0101 (412) 578 2272

Details: The School of Urban and Public Affairs was founded in 1968 through a grant of $10 million from Mr and Mrs Richard K. Mellon. Pittsburgh is protected by the most stringent anti-pollution code in the USA and offers a range of cultural, sporting and recreational facilities.

Admissions Officer: Victoria Salco.

Placement Officer: Ed Mosier.

Courses Offered and Duration: MS (2 years, including compulsory summer internship)
PhD (4 years for students with bachelor's degree).

Fees: $9,850. Estimated total annual cost: $17,000 (1984).

Admissions Criteria: Some previous business experience preferred. GMAT required as well as a bachelor's degree. Personal interview preferred.

Specialties: Strong on quantitative methods, systems and operational research.

Staff: 32.

Teaching Styles Used: Varied according to the nature of the course material.

Assessment: Continuous assessment.

Source of Student Finance: BGA loan scheme available.

Other Information: Close relationship with Carnegie Institute of Technology and other graduate schools.

UNIVERSITY OF CHICAGO
Graduate School of Business,
1101 E. 58th Street, Chicago, Illinois 60637
Tel.: 0101 (312) 962 7369

Details: The Graduate School of Business was founded in 1898. The Chicago approach is to teach the basic disciplines which underlie business operations and their applications in business management and to conduct basic research which will contribute to the understanding and solution of business problems. Participating in the Internship Programme are about 70 companies which offer first-year students the opportunity to work for them. The Placement Office hosted 11,000 interviews between graduates and several hundred companies in 1984.

Admissions Officer: Kevin Martin, Director of Admissions, Graduate School of Business.

Placement Officer: Barbara McGloin, Director of Placement, Graduate School of Business.

Courses Offered and Duration: MBA (18 months, 870 enrolments 1984).
PhD (approx. 4 years, 82 enrolments).

Fees: US citizens: $10,450. Overseas students: $10,450. Estimated total annual cost: $17,500 for 1984/5.

Admissions Criteria: Qualifications in economics, calculus, and computer programming recommended. GMAT required, no formal cut-off. Outstanding academic record and personal leadership qualities important.

Business Experience of Current Students: 50% of students generally have business experience.

Specialties: Accounting, finance, marketing, operations research/management science, economics and many others.

Staff: 112 faculty members.

Teaching Styles Used: Lectures and class discussions; class size is about 35 students.

Assessment: Formal examinations, written reports, group projects, dissertations in the PhD programme; subjects usually have formal examinations mid-term and end of term.

Class Hours Per Week: 13 hours.

Source of Student Finance: About 5% of all MBA students get fellowships or scholarships, usually close to full fees. Loans are occasionally available to second-year foreign students to the value of full tuition. PhD students are judged individually for financial assistance. BGA loan scheme available.

Student Composition: 16% overseas students, 22% women students.

Other Information: MBA students may enter the programme at any quarter of the year; however, most begin in either the Summer (June), or the Autumn (September) quarters and take 3 to 4 courses per quarter, completing 20 courses for the MBA. The school maintains an International Business Exchange Programme with the London School of Economics and Political Science, the London School of Graduate Business Studies, the Catholic University of Leuven, the Université Catholique de Louvain, and St Gall Graduate School of Economics, Business and Public Administration and Essec (Paris).

COLUMBIA UNIVERSITY
**Graduate School of Business, 105 Uris Hall,
Columbia University, New York, New York 10027
Tel.: 0101 (212) 280 5567**

Details: Columbia University is situated in the Morningside Heights area of New York City near the Hudson River; it offers an MBA and PhD programme. There are approximately 10 UK students per year in the programme. The School operates on a three term system – students may begin their enrolment in any of the three terms of the academic year, and continue their studies without interruption until they graduate.

Admissions Officer: Joyce Cornell. (The Placement Office scheduled over 10,000 individual interviews for the class of 1984.)

Courses Offered and Duration: MBA programme (2 years, 600 enrolments) with a choice of concentrations in the following: Accounting, Business Economics and Public Policy, Corporate Relations and Public Affairs, Finance, International Business, Management of Organisations, Management Science, Marketing, Money and Financial Markets, Operations Management, Public and Nonprofit Management.
PhD – Main aim is preparation for a career in academic research and teaching.
There is also an organisation run by MBA students – MBA Management Consultants – which works with small businesses in Manhattan, providing educational opportunities for its members through consulting assignments, training programmes and guest lectures.

Fees: $5,270 per term (1984). Estimated cost to UK students: $7,500 per term, including $3,000 for room/board/books/expenses.

Admissions Criteria: Bachelor's degree, academic transcripts, GMAT score, references.

Teaching Styles Used: Lectures, conferences, case studies, discussions, student research.

Source of Student Finance: Some fellowships. Loan finance is also available but only in the second year. BGA loan scheme available.

CORNELL UNIVERSITY
Graduate School of Business and Public Administration,
Ithaca, New York 14853
Tel.: 0101 (607) 256 2327

Details: The Graduate School of Business and Public Administration at Cornell was founded in 1946. It also includes the Sloan Programme of Hospital and Health Services Administration.

Admissions Officer: Maria Blackburn, 313 Malott Hall, Cornell University, Ithaca, New York 14853.

Placement Officer: Albert Brill, 311 Malott Hall, Cornell University, Ithaca, New York 14853.

Courses Offered and Duration: MBA (2 years, 240 enrolments). Students choose one of nine areas of concentration. Overall there are some 105 individual courses.

Fees: $10,250. Estimated cost to UK students per annum: $17,000 (1984).

Admissions Criteria: Preferred age 23–35. Business experience of 2–5 years ideal though not essential. Good academic record very important with mathematics through introductory calculus essential. GMAT required plus high degree of motivation, leadership potential, etc.

Business Experience of Current Students: 30% with 1–3 months vacation experience; 20% with 1–2 years experience; 25% with 2–5 years experience; 8% with 5 or more years experience.

Specialties: Finance, accounting, operations research and production, marketing, organisational theory.

Staff: 44 teaching staff, most of whom engage in external consultancy.

Teaching Styles Used: Case studies, group and class discussions, lectures, tutorials, computer work, projects.

Assessment: Principally formal examinations, group projects and dissertation. Informal tests once a month in first year, formal examinations twice a term first and second years.

Class Hours Per Week: Total work load: 64 hours approx.

Source of Student Finance: BGA loan scheme available.

DARTMOUTH COLLEGE,
Amos Tuck School of Business Administration,
Hanover, New Hampshire 03755

Details: Tuck School, founded in 1900, is the oldest graduate school of business in the US. From its inception, the Master's degree has been the only degree offered by the Tuck School. The following facilities are adjacent to one another and connected by underground corridors: Tuck Hall (offices, classrooms, etc.), Murdough Centre (completed in 1973 – classrooms of advanced design, library, computer facilities, small group study rooms), 3 dormitories, Stell Dining Hall. Attractive duplex housing facilities for married students are located close to Hanover. Cultural and athletic facilities of the College are available to Tuck students.

Admissions Officer: Director of Admissions and Student Affairs.

Placement Officer: Director of Career Counselling and Placement.

Courses Offered and Duration: MBA programme (18 months, 165 enrolments).

Fees: US students $10,540. Overseas students: $10,540. Estimated total annual cost: $17,500 (1984).

Admissions Criteria: Preferred age: 22–30. Business experience of 2+ years preferred. Bachelor's degree, any major. Some study in maths and economics recommended. GMAT required with a score of 560 desirable, no cut-off score. 2 faculty and/or employer letters of recommendation, grades, essays – for content and writing skills – also important.

Business Experience of Current Students: 65% have had 1 or more years of work.

Specialties: General management curriculum.

Staff: 32 full-time lecturing staff in school.

Teaching Styles Used: Cases, lectures, discussions, business games.

Assessment: Quizzes, class participation, examinations, papers through the term.

Class Hours Per Week: 12+.

Source of Student Finance: Foreign applicants are urged to explore opportunities available from their government and private sources, as the school is generally unable to provide funds for foreign nationals. BGA loan scheme available.

Student Composition: 7% overseas students, 23% women students.

Other Information: Application deadline April 15.

HARVARD UNIVERSITY
Graduate School of Business Administration, Boston, Massachusetts
Tel.: 0101 (617) 495 6127

Details: The Graduate School of Business Administration was founded in 1908. Emphasising the practical rather than the theoretical approach to problems confronting managers, teaching is based on the case study method of instruction. The Business School, which is situated on the south bank of the Charles River, has a unique, self-contained campus located in the Boston-Cambridge community.

Admissions Officer: John Lynch, Director, MBA Admissions Board, Morgan Hall, HBS, Soldiers Field, Boston, MA.

Placement Officer: Parker Llewellyn.

Courses Offered and Duration: MBA programme (2 years, 860 enrolments 1984).
DBA programme (1–3 years, 88 enrolments).

Fees: $10,000. Estimated total annual cost: $18,000.

Admissions Criteria: Business experience of 2 years or more is desirable. BA or equivalent usually required. GMAT required. Grade point average or equivalent extracurricular activities; written application; recommendations also important.

Business Experience of Current Students: Approximately 90% of students have worked 2 years or more in business or government.

Specialties: General management.

Staff: 250 faculty members and 10 from other schools teaching on programmes.

Teaching Styles Used: Principally case study, supplemented by written exams and papers, a management game, readings, etc.

Assessment: 50% class participation, written mid-terms and finals in most courses.

Class Hours Per Weeks: 20.

Source of Student Finance: Some school fellowships plus Federal and school loans are available to students with demonstrated need. BGA loan scheme available.

Student Composition: 20% overseas students, 22% women students.

UNIVERSITY OF ILLINOIS
Department of Business Administration, 219 Commerce West, University of Illinois, Urbana, Illinois 61801

Details: The MBA programme is designed especially to meet the educational needs of students preparing for a variety of administrative positions. It is designed so that superior students from many areas of undergraduate study will be able to achieve a rigorous educational background in business administration within two years. The purpose of the MBA programme is first to develop and then to apply fundamental concepts and methods in the quantitative, social and behavioural sciences to problems in administrative decision-making.

Admissions Officer: Director Admissions and Student Affairs.

Courses Offered and Duration: MBA: a range of 16-week courses in organisational behaviour, marketing, operations, economics and accounting is available.
MBA – executive MBA (one day a week).

Fees: Illinois residents: $1,125. Non-residents $5,240. Estimated total cost for a foreign student: $12,850.

Admissions Criteria: Completion of Bachelor's degree. GMAT required with a minimum score of 550. B average undergraduate education, personal statement, 3 letters of recommendation also required.

Specialties: Marketing, management science, organisational behaviour, management information systems, international business, business economics, strategic planning.

Staff: 46 full-time lecturing staff in school.

Teaching Styles Used: Case studies, lectures, simulations, projects, discussion.

Assessment: Dependent upon course and professor.

Class Hours Per Week: 4 per course.

Source of Student Finance: Limited opportunities for financial aid depending upon performance and need. BGA loan scheme available.

Student Composition: 10% overseas students, 20% women students.

INDIANA UNIVERSITY
Bloomington, Indiana 47405

Details: The Graduate School of Business was founded in 1936 and is now one of the top national business schools. The graduate business curriculum offers a strong core curriculum whose flow from basic disciplines to business functions to environmental integration provides a sound foundation for general management. The school is located in Bloomington about 50 miles south of Indianapolis. Living costs in Bloomington are substantially lower than in the major cities, and cultural and recreational activities in the area are plentiful. Students have access to a literary collection that ranks fourth in size among US university libraries, as well as extensive research and computer facilities. Students may live on-campus in graduate residence halls, or off-campus in local apartments or houses.

Admissions Officer: Office of Admissions, Student Services Building.

Courses Offered and Duration: MBA (2 years).
DBA (3 years).
MBA/JD (4 years).

Fees: Overseas students: $185 per credit hour. Students will normally enroll 24 credit hours per academic year. Estimated total annual cost for an overseas single student is about $9,500.

Admissions Criteria: Undergraduate degree. GMAT is required. Although there is no minimum required score, the average entering student placed in the 80th percentile. Admissions Committee looks for past academic performance equivalent to a 3.2 grade point average (US scale). Candidates are also evaluated on extra-curricular activities, community service, work experience, career objectives, and letters of recommendation. Application deadline is April 15 for fall entry and November 1 for January entrance.

Business Experience of Current Students: 55% have had 1 year or more full-time work experience.

Specialties: Finance, marketing, management and administration, accounting, international business, MIS, operations management, quantitative business analysis.

Staff: A full-time faculty of 160, many internationally known with demonstrated teaching excellence and scholarship in diversified areas of business.

Teaching Styles Used: Predominantly the case method. Business simulation games, lectures, seminars, discussion groups are also used.

Assessment: Class participation and discussion; tests and written reports. A minimum of one mid-term examination and one final examination in each course each semester. Substantial work in teams during the second year.

Class Hours Per Week: 12.

Source of Student Finance: Graduate assistantships, fellowships, loans. BGA loan scheme available.

Student Composition: 15% overseas students representing 46 foreign countries, 23% women students.

Other Information: Student intake: 250 in the autumn, 100 in the spring.

UNIVERSITY OF KANSAS
202 Summerfield Hall, Lawrence, Kansas
Tel.: 0101 (913) 864 2700

Details: The School of Business was organised in 1924. Graduate programmes are accredited by the American Assembly of Collegiate Schools of Business. The University is located 40 miles west of Kansas City. Library contains over 2 million volumes with extensive research facilities and computation centre.

Admissions Officer: Director of Masters Programmes.

Courses Offered and Duration: MBA (60 hours, 380 enrolments 1984).
MS (30 hours, 32 enrolments).
PhD (24–48 months, 30 enrolments).
MBA/JD (118 hours, 42 enrolments).

Fees: Kansas residents: $1,125. Non-residents: $3,850. Estimated total annual cost: $5,000–9,000.

Admissions Criteria: Business experience preferred, but not required. Baccalaureate degree, any field: 3.0 preferred. GMAT required with a preferred score of 480. Extra-curricular activities, organisation participation, leadership also important.

Business Experience of Current Students: From 0 to more than 20 years; average years of experience 2.7.

Specialties: Major areas of courses offering accounting, finance, labour relations, marketing, operations research, organisation and administration.

Staff: 63 full-time lecturing staff in school with 1 from other schools teaching on programmes and 3 from industrial/commercial organisations.

Teaching Styles Used: Lecture, group discussion, case studies, business games, computer simulations.

Assessment: Exams, research papers, class participation, case analysis. 2–3 per semester.

Class Hours Per Week: 15.

Source of Student Finance: Financial aid, campus work, off-campus work. BGA loan scheme available.

Student Composition: 6.9% overseas students, 26.7% women students.

Other Information: Special programmes leading to combined MBA/JD and MS in petroleum management.

MASSACHUSETTS INSTITUTE OF TECHNOLOGY
Sloan School of Management, MIT, Cambridge, Massachusetts 02139
Tel.: 0101 (617) 253 3730

Details: The Sloan School of Management develops students who will take on leadership roles in important organisations. Students acquire confidence in managerial decision-making through a flexible management curriculum that stresses theoretical and applied studies as well as practical exposure to management problems in private and public organisations. The Boston area is rich in museums, libraries, theatres, etc. Accommodation on campus is available for about half the single students but is scarce for married students.

Admissions Officer: Dr. Geof A. Barks, Masters Programme Admissions Director, 50 Memorial Drive.

Placement Officer: Linda Stantial, Director of Placement, 50 Memorial Drive.

Courses Offered and Duration: Sloan Masters Programme (2 academic years, 200 enrolments 1984).
Accelerated Masters Programme (12 months, 50 enrolments).

Fees: Sloan Masters annual fees for all students: $10,500. Accelerated Masters annual fees for all students: $15,800. Estimated total annual cost: $17,000– 25,000.

Admissions Criteria: Ideally, business experience of 1–5 years, 1 year of economics and calculus. GMAT required with a score of at least 500. Strong motivation and leadership potential, academic record, business experience and letters of recommendation.

Business Experience of Current Students: 23% with vacation experience only; 28% with 1–2 years experience; 23% with 3–4 years experience; and 26% with 5 or more years.

Specialties: Financing, accounting and control, management information systems, organisational studies.

Staff: 71 full-time lecturing staff, 6 visiting staff.

Teaching Styles Used: Varied.

Assessment: Formal examinations every three months, term papers and Master's thesis, informal tests once a week in core subjects of 1 year programme, once a month in 2 year programme.

Source of Student Finance: Loans, rarely more than $8,000 per annum, also part-time assistantships but not for entering students. BGA loan scheme available.

Student Composition: 26% overseas students, 23% women students.

UNIVERSITY OF MICHIGAN
Graduate School of Business Administration,
Ann Arbor, Michigan
Tel.: 0101 (313) 764 1817

Details: Teaching of accounting and business subjects began in 1889 and the University of Michigan was a founding member of the American Association of Collegiate Schools of Business in 1919. The school was established as an independent academic unit of the university in 1924. Ann Arbor is a large university-orientated community providing a pleasant environment close to major industrial and commercial centres. Social, cultural and athletic advantages are considerable.

Admissions Officer: Office of Admissions and Student Services.

Placement Officer: Placement Office.

Courses Offered and Duration: MBA (2 academic years, 800 enrolments 1984).
PhD (3 academic years, 100 enrolments).

Fees: US citizens: $6,800. Overseas students: $6,800. Estimated total annual cost: $12,500 per academic year of 8 months.

Admissions Criteria: Preferred age 22–35. Business experience considered favourably but not required. Mathematics and economics (basic introductory study). GMAT required with a score of, on average, 600. Involvement in school, community, and professional activities also important.

Business Experience of Current Students: 45% have substantial full-time work experience.

Staff: Full-time regular faculty of 95 professors.

Teaching Styles Used: Varied, with considerable emphasis on case study, co-operative group activities and contact with business organisations.

Assessment: Considerable written and oral presentations required with regular evaluation in each course. No thesis or comprehensive examinations.

Class Hours Per Week: 15.

Source of Student Finance: Personal funds primarily. BGA loan scheme available.

Student Composition: 10% overseas students, 30% women students.

NEW YORK UNIVERSITY
Graduate School of Business Administration,
New York University,
100 Trinity Place, New York City, New York 10006
Tel.: 0101 (212) 285 6000

Details: One of the oldest graduate management schools in the USA, GBA has long served the business community in the Metropolitan New York area and has increased in prominence both nationally and internationally. There is convenient rapid transit to all locations in New York City; dormitory and apartment accommodations in the historic Greenwich Village area.

Admissions Officer: Jane de Vos.

Placement Officer: Cathleen Kennedy.

Courses Offered and Duration: MBA programme (2 years, 1,000 enrolments in 1984, 3 years part-time, 3,000 enrolments).
PhD programme (4 years, 300 enrolments).
MS in Quantitative Analysis programme (varied length, 30 enrolments).
Advanced Professional Certificate (varied length, 325 enrolments).

Fees: About $8,000. Estimated total annual cost about $17,000.

Admissions Criteria: Preferred age 22–35. Business experience desirable but none required. Any bachelor's degree or acceptable equivalent. GMAT required. The Committee on Admissions stresses that its evaluation of applicants is thorough and comprehensive. Accordingly, relative weight of criteria can vary among applicants. Approximately 30% of applicants accepted.

Business Experience of Current Students: Average level of business experience is 3–4 years.

Specialties: Finance, accounting, international business; flexible integrated curriculum; wide interaction with New York business community.

Staff: 185. More than half of the faculty maintain ties with the business community as consultants, board members and partners in local firms.

Teaching Styles Used: Comprehensive. Includes business theory, case study method and simulated business experience.

Assessment: Varies from course to course. Can include papers or written cases plus mid-term and final examinations.

Class Hours Per Week: Average is approximately 12.

USA

Source of Student Finance: Loans, fellowships (usually not available to international students during the first year of study), graduate assistantships. BGA loan scheme available.

Student Composition: 18% overseas students, 45% women students.

J. L. KELLOGG GRADUATE SCHOOL OF MANAGEMENT, NORTHWESTERN UNIVERSITY
Leverone Hall, Evanston, Illinois 60201
Tel.: 0101 (312) 492 3300

Details: The School of Commerce was founded in 1908 and became the J.L. Kellogg Graduate School of Management in 1979. It is located on the shore of Lake Michigan, twelve miles north of Chicago's business district in the 170 acre campus of Northwestern University. Leverone Hall is a six-floor modern building, housing classrooms, lounges, computer and behaviour science laboratories, faculty and administrative offices; student housing is within walking distance.

Admissions Officer: Director of Admissions.

Placement Officer: Director of Placement and Career Counselling.

Courses Offered and Duration: MM (24 months, 850 enrolments 1984).
PhD (36 months, 92 enrolments).

Fees: US citizens: $9,800 per year. Foreign students $9,800 per year. Estimated annual cost: $17,000.

Admission Criteria: Preferred age 22–35. Business experience recommended. Baccalaureate degree. Work in economics and mathematics encouraged. GMAT required. 2 letters of recommendation. Certificate of Financial Responsibility also important.

Business Experience of Current Students: About 60% of the class has full-time working experience.

Specialties: MM degrees in business, hospital and health services, public administration and transportation. Concentrations available in 12 functional areas including accounting, finance, marketing, organisation behaviour, international business, etc.

108

Staff: 110 faculty members.

Teaching Styles Used: The teaching approach is a mixed one utilising lectures, cases, field studies, oral presentations, class participation and mid-term examinations as well.

Class Hours Per Week: 13 hours.

Source of Student Finance: Northwestern does not have resources to aid foreign students in financing their MM programmes. BGA loan scheme available.

Student Composition: 15% overseas students, 28% women students.

PACE UNIVERSITY
Graduate School of Business, Pace Plaza,
New York, New York 10038

Details: The University, founded in 1906, is a private coeducational institution with 3 campuses in lower Manhattan, Pleasantville and White Plains. The Graduate School was founded in 1958, became a separate school in 1963 and was eventually reorganised in 1977 to form the Graduate School of Business.

Courses Offered and Duration: MBA, MS and DPS programmes in a wide variety of fields are available at all three campuses.
The following joint programmes are also available.
JD/MBA in conjuction with the University's School of Law.
MBA/MS in Urban Planning in conjunction with the Pratt Institute.
Joint Master's and Doctoral programme in Economics in conjunction with the State University of New York at Stoney Brook.
Joint MBA programme in conjunction with the École Supérieure de Commerce de Lyon in France.

Admissions Officer: Director of Admissions.

Fees: Tuition $185 per credit. Application fee: $20. Dormitory rooms: $ 1,800 per academic year.

Admissions Criteria: Bachelor's degree in any field. GMAT required. Academic record, letters of recommendation, interview, etc. also taken into consideration. TOEFL required from those whose native language is not English.

Staff: Faculty of 56.

Assessment: To qualify the following requirements must be satisfied: MBA – 39- to 62-credit course requirement; MS – a 36-credit course requirement; DPS – a 55-credit requirement, three-field written and oral qualifying examinations, and a dissertation and defense. For the MBA a minimum of 33 credits must be successfully completed in residence at the GSB.

Source of Student Finance: A number of graduate scholarships and assistantships are available awarded on the basis of outstanding scholarship and demonstrated financial need. BGA loan scheme available.

Other Information: Research facilities accessible to students include the virtually unlimited library resources of both University and the New York City area, and the University's Univac 1106 computer. The Graduate School of Business's Centre for Applied Research, Institute for Economic Research, and Institute for International Finance also offer opportunities for research.

UNIVERSITY OF PENNSYLVANIA
Wharton Graduate Division, The Wharton School, 102 Vance Hall, CS, University of Pennsylvania, Philadelphia 19104

Details: The Wharton School was founded in 1881 and is the oldest collegiate school of business in the world. The Graduate Division was started in 1921. Vance Hall, the home of Wharton Graduate Division, was completed in late 1972.

Admissions Officer: Director of Admissions.

Placement Officer: Director of Placement.

Courses Offered: MBA.

Fees: US citizens: $8,750. Overseas students: $8,750. Estimated total annual cost: $17,000.

Admissions Criteria: Preferred age 22–35 years. Business experience of several years is desirable. Bachelor's degree. Calculus helpful. GMAT required. Academic record, experience, activities, motivation, as well as leadership also important.

Specialties: Finance, operations research, accounting, management science, multinational enterprise, health care.

Staff: 20 lecturing staff, most of whom engage in external consulting.

Teaching Styles Used: Lectures, case studies, classroom particpation and consulting projects, business games.

Assessment: At least one examination each semester, with 75% of classes requiring a final examination.

Class Hours Per Week: 15 hours.

Source of Student Finance: UK students are eligible for Thouron Scholarships which number about 25 yearly and are tenable in any division of the University of Pennsylvania. BGA loan scheme available.

Student Composition: 19% overseas students.

UNIVERSITY OF PITTSBURGH
Graduate School of Business, University of Pittsburgh, Pittsburgh, Pennsylvania 15260

Details: The School has granted degrees in business since 1908, and became the Graduate School of Business in 1960, accredited by the American Assembly of Collegiate Schools of Business. The University of Pittsburgh is an urban campus with over 25,000 students and various research and professional centres. Pittsburgh is the third largest corporate headquarters city in the US, national and area firms often sending representatives to campus.

Admissions Officer: Director of Admissions.

Placement Officer: Director of Placement.

Courses Offered and Duration: MBA (11 months).
PhD.

Fees: Foreign students' tuition $8,320. Estimated other expenses: $9,000. Total estimated expenses: $17,320.

Admissions Criteria: Business experience recommended but not required. BA/BS or equivalent. GMAT required. Recommendation letters, 1 course in integral and differential calculus are required.

Business Experience of Current Students: 50% of class (full-time MBA) has at least one year of experience.

Specialties: Accounting/finance, marketing, operations research, strategic planning, management information systems, behavioural science in business.

Staff: 67 full-time lecturing staff in school, 1 from other school teaching on programmes and several from industrial/commercial organisations.

Teaching Styles Used: All methods used.

Assessment: One examination mid-term and a final examination for each course.

Class Hours Per Week: 18.

Source of Student Finance: MBA programme: none available for foreign students. PhD programme: Fellowships and Research Assistantships available. BGA loan scheme available.

Student Composition: 10% overseas students, 31% women students.

Other Information: 11 month MBA programme begins in September, graduates the following August. Rolling admission process, early application advised.

UNIVERSITY OF SOUTHERN CALIFORNIA
Graduate School of Business, University Park, Los Angeles, California 90007
Tel.: 0101 (213) 743 2424

Details: Founded in 1880, the University is the oldest major private co-educational university in the west. The University is a member of the American Association of Universities. The School is accredited by the American Assembly of Collegiate Schools of Business. USC is located in the heart of the downtown Los Angeles area, the third largest city in the United States, and is known for its close ties with the surrounding business community.

Admissions Officer: Director of Admissions and Recruitment; Director of PhD Programme.

Placement Officer: Director of Career Services.

Courses Offered and Duration: MBA (24 months, 1,400 enrolments in 1984).
PhD (36 months, 180 enrolments).
MS in Management Studies (18 months).
MS in Organisational Behaviour.

Fees: Californian residents: $7,425. Non-residents: $7,425. Estimated total annual cost: $17,000.

Admissions Criteria: Preferred age 24–30. Business experience recommended and encouraged. Mathematics and economics, GMAT and TOEFL required. Letters of recommendation, statement of purpose for graduate study, letter of financial support also important.

Business Experience of Current Students: Average 24 months full-time work experience.

Specialties: International finance, real estate, investments, organisational behaviour, marketing.

Staff: 135 faculty, 100 from other schools teaching on programmes and 115 from industrial/commercial organisations.

Teaching Styles Used: Case studies, lectures, simulation, business games.

Assessment: At least 2 exams; mid-term and final plus papers and oral reports.

Class Hours Per Week: 4.

Source of Student Finance: International students must fund their education and provide evidence of financial support.

Student Composition: 17% overseas students, 41% women students.

STANFORD UNIVERSITY
Graduate School of Business, Stanford, California 94305
Tel.: 0101 (415) 497 2766

Details: Adjacent to Palo Alto 35 miles from San Francisco, the School was founded in 1925. There are on-campus student apartments, eating clubs, all amenities available at university and locally.

Admissions Officer: Kathleen M. Gwynne, Director MBA Admissions.

Placement Officer: Ayse Kenmore.

Courses Offered and Duration: MBA (2 years, 325 enrolments 1984).
PhD (1–5 years, 14 enrolments).
MS Executive Sloan Programme – company sponsored (1 year, 100 enrolments).

Fees: US citizens: $10,056 (1984). Overseas students: $10,056. Estimated total annual cost: $18,000.

Admissions Criteria: All information for MBA programme only. General age range 21–41, median age 26. Business experience of 1 or more years preferred. Bachelor's honours degree – 1st class or upper 2nd. GMAT required.

Business Experience of Current Students: Class of 1984 – 78% had 1 or more years experience.

Specialties: Public management programme, health services administration.

Staff: 82 full-time lecturing staff in school, 4 from other schools teaching on programmes and 11 from industrial/commercial organisations.

Teaching Styles Used: Case studies, lectures, computer simulations, team assignments.

Assessment: Examinations and papers.

Class Hours Per Week: 20.

Source of Student Finance: Limited number of Fellowships for portion of tuition only. BGA loan scheme available.

Student Composition: 16% overseas students, 26% women students.

UNIVERSITY OF VIRGINIA
The Colgate Darden Graduate School of Business Administration,
Box 6550, Charlottesville, Virginia 22906
Tel.: 0101 (804) 924 0311

Details: The School has a 25 year history with alumni in all 50 states, District of Columbia and in 28 foreign countries. The University of Virginia was chartered in 1819 under a sponsorship of Thomas Jefferson. Charlottesville is a city of 44,000 within sight of the Blue Ridge Mountains. The Campus was designed by Jefferson.

Admissions Officer: Director of Admissions.

Courses Offered and Duration: MBA (2 year programme, 180 enrolments 1984).
DBA (1/2 years, 17 enrolments). Total duration: 42 months.

Fees: Virginians: $3,100 (1984). Other students: $5,210. Estimated total annual cost $13,000 for other students.

Admissions Criteria: Average age 25. Some previous business experience preferred. Bachelor's degree required, as well as GMAT. Advanced standing is possible allowing minimal completion time of two semesters.

Business Experience of Previous Students: 60% liberal arts background, 80% with military and/or work experience since graduation.

Specialties: Attached Institutes of Applied Ethics, Banking Studies, Financial Analysis.

Staff: 56. Two senior industrialists appointed as visiting lecturers.

Teaching Styles: Most courses taught using case method although other methods used where appropriate.

Assessment: Formal grades determined at the end of first year rather than individual semester grades. Second year assessment by course and elective credits, a written report and a written case.

Class Hours Per Week: Total workload 60–80 hours. Classes 25 hours per week.

Source of Student Finance: Scholarships and loans available. No financial assistance is available for first year foreign students. BGA loan scheme available.

Student Composition: 4% overseas students, 27% women students.

Other Information: Relatively small intake with strong Virgina connections.

The Business Graduates Association Ltd

WHAT IS THE BGA?

The BGA is an independent non-profit-making organisation. It was founded in 1967 by a group of British business graduates, with the aim of advancing business education for the benefit of the production sector of British society and for increased efficiency in other sectors. Today the BGA has 2,800 individual and 150 corporate members and undertakes a wide range of activities in support of the aim. The CBI, the BIM and Government have warmly endorsed its work.

WHO CAN JOIN?

Anyone can become an individual member who holds or is in process of acquiring a postgraduate business degree, doctorate, or Sloan Fellowship from a business school in the BGA list, provided they work in Britain or for a British company abroad. Any company or organisation can become a corporate member by subscribing to BGA funds.

WHAT DOES THE BGA DO?

The activities of the BGA are designed to ensure:

(a) that industry, commerce, and the public sector receive value for the money invested in the business schools, through effective use of their products;

(b) that the courses offered by the business schools are practical, relevant, and of high quality;

(c) that the maximum number of suitably qualified people seek business education;

(d) that anti-business propaganda aimed at young people is effectively countered.

In pursuing its mission the Association has one unique advantage: all its members hold postgraduate business qualifications which they are putting to practical use. This allows the BGA to identify from experience the research which is needed, to choose the best means of communicating the results to industry, to the business schools, and to students, and to provide practical assistance in taking action.

The services provided by the BGA flow from this work. They overlap at many points. They are of immediate practical value to members, both individual and corporate; and they are all ultimately beneficial to the economy.

WHAT THE BGA OFFERS CORPORATE MEMBERS

The BGA publishes and provides free of charge to corporate members a variety of handbooks and reports based on research carried out by the Association. The subjects covered include business school programmes, attitudinal studies and salary surveys, and matters of current interest to the business community. The material can be supplemented by in-company conferences at corporate members' request.

To reduce the expense and man hours involved in recruitment, the BGA provides a placement service for corporate members. This consists of a broadsheet circulated at once and at minimal cost to all BGA members whenever a company wants to advertise a post which may need a business graduate. A single successful use of this can save a corporate member twenty times its annual subscription or more.

Although there are now several thousand business graduates working in Britain many companies still have no experience of employing them. The BGA therefore offers assistance both in its published material and by free consultation on the effective use of business graduates and the particular functions in which they can contribute most.

The needs and views of corporate members are continuously studied, analysed, and transmitted to the schools by the BGA through its membership of business liaison committees at the business schools, and through their alumni. The BGA makes additional arrangements to cater for the special needs of business schools in the corporate members list.

In addition to its familiarity with the postgraduate field, the BGA has considerable resources of knowledge and experience in many other matters connected with management development and management education generally. Theses are always available to corporate members on request to the BGA office, and any particular requirement which companies may have can usually be satisfied at short notice.

Corporate members receive BGA periodicals and the address book published annually, with details of members by industry, function, geographical area and business school. By this means, and by participating in the various conferences arranged at intervals by the Association, companies can establish and maintain contacts at every level.

WHAT THE BGA OFFERS INDIVIDUAL MEMBERS

As a professional association the BGA provides its members with a forum and a means of making and maintaining contact with fellow business graduates and senior management in other fields. It also keeps members in touch through its quarterly magazine with topics and trends in management and business education and with the work, achievements, and policy of the Association.

The BGA has a mission for the common good, and its members have the distinction of contributing to it, through speaking, writing, and research, in which all members are encouraged to participate. Moreover, the Association has a reputation for insistence on quality, established by the work and calibre of its members, which enables it to exert an influence out of proportion to its size. A study of the services offered to corporate members will show that individual members are involved in most of them and benefit accordingly.

Meetings are arranged for members at frequent intervals, with a mixed professional and social flavour, the accent being on the former.

Although the placement service provided by the BGA is for the benefit of corporate members, its value to individual members is obvious; additional lines of communication on this subject run through the BGA office.

BGA SERVICES TO NON-MEMBERS

The BGA was founded to serve a national interest. To generate the means of doing so in terms both of finance and of work in the field, it offers services to its members in return for their interest and support. With these it is able to provide services for people and institutions outside the membership which further its aims and justify its charitable status.

The BGA arranges free public counselling sessions for the same market in spring and autumn, with recent graduates on hand to answer questions, and puts interested people in touch with graduates of particular schools. The Association arranges low-interest loans to help experienced executives to finance their courses; the total of loans arranged under this scheme is now approaching £2,000,000.

An additional service in the educational field is the organisation of BGA speakers to visit schools and universities throughout Britain to discuss and illustrate the merits of a career in industry and to counter the anti-business propaganda to which young people are exposed.

The resources and publications of the Association are available to Regional Management Centres, Polytechnics and educational establishments at every level. It is a cardinal principle of BGA policy that children should be taught the economic facts of national life throughout their schooldays; it is self-evident that the success of the BGA mission to modernise management and improve productivity will be accelerated in proportion as this is done.

Through its independence and wide variation in the experience and employment of its members, the BGA is able to make objective studies and surveys of matters of importance to the economy. Typical reports produced have covered Planning Agreements, the National Health Service, Local Government, Industrial Democracy, Production Management, and Smaller Businesses, and these have been made available to Government Departments, Members of Parliament and the public.

The Association maintains links and exchanges published material with other institutions whose interests and activities are related. These include the Foundation for Management Education, the British Institute of Management, the Conference of University Management Schools, the Confederation of British Industry and the Trade Union movement.

Since the business schools were founded in the middle 1960s the public debate on the employment of their products and the merits of their programmes has not always been well informed. The BGA has set itself to correct misapprehension by suppling factual information and balanced argument through its reports and its contributions to the media. This activity has had beneficial results and is likely to be required for the foreseeable future.

PUBLICATIONS OF THE BGA

The Business Graduate. The quarterly journal of the Association.
The Business Graduate in Britain. An attitudinal and statistical study – latest edition 1979, £3.00.
Business Graduates – Some Attitudes towards Business Schools, 1976. A survey of business school programmes with recommendations for

future development, based on the views of 835 business graduates in the light of their own work experience.

Remuneration of Business Graduates, 1976. An analysis of 835 questionnaires completed by BGA members.

Planning Agreement? Practical Considerations. A report which answers the question "If we had to do it, what would it be like?".

Education for Senior Health Services Management. Examines the requirement to provides a masters degree level course for higher managers in the Health Service.

Education for Senior Local Government Officers. Examines the requirement to provide a masters degree level course for higher officers.

Higher Management Education and the Production Function. Analyses the present image of the production function and suggests methods of achieving greater efficiency and improved career prospects.

Successful Production Management. A follow-up study. £7.50.

A-Level Business Studies in the United Kingdom. A study of progress over the past 14 years.

Small Firms – A Fair Crack of the Whip. A review of the smaller business sector since the Bolton Report, with recommendations.

Small Firms – The Successful Spin-Off. How large firms can hive off divisions or departments. £7.50. Summary £3.50.

1981 Survey of Business Graduates in the UK. 1982. £7.50.

Business School Education in the 1980s. 1982. £3.50.

Education for Business Communicators. 1982. £3.50.

The BGA List of Courses at UK Business Schools and Universities

*Denotes approved courses giving eligibility for membership of the BGA.

University of Aston
 *MBA   All courses.
 *MSc   Operational Research, Personnel Management, Public Sector Management, Systems Analysis.
  Diploma in Business Administration, Personnel Management, Public Sector Management.

University of Bath
 *MSc   Business Administration, Industrial Marketing, Industrial Relations.

Queen's University of Belfast (Department of Business Studies)
 *MBA   All courses.
  Diploma in Business Administration.

University of Bradford Management Centre
 *MBA   All courses.
  Diploma Management and Administration.

City University Business School
 *MBA   All courses.
 *MSc   Business Systems and Analysis.
  Diploma in Systems Analysis.

Cranfield School of Management, Institute of Technology
 *MBA   All courses.
 *MSc   Industrial Management.
  Diploma Industrial Management.

Durham University Business School
*MSc   Management Studies, all courses.

University of Edinburgh
*MBA   All courses.
*MPhil
  DipBA

University of Glasgow
*MBA   All courses.
*MEng   Engineering Management.
*MLitt   Management Studies.

Henley   The Management College
*MBA   All courses.
*MSc   Management Studies, all courses.

University of Hull
*MA   Management Systems, all courses.
*MSc   Management Sciences, all courses.

University of Lancaster (School of Management)
  MA   Accounting and Finance, Business Analysis, Marketing,
    Organisational Psychology, Systems in Management, Manage-
    ment Learning.
*MSc   Operational Research.
  Diploma in Operational Research, Business Analysis.

University of Leeds (Department of Management Studies)
*MBA

London Graduate School of Business
*MSc   Business Studies, all courses.
*London Sloan Fellowship Programme.

London School of Economics (LSE)
*MSc in Business Studies
  Diploma in Business Studies.

University of London, Imperial College
*MSc   Management Science.
  Diploma Management Science.

Loughborough University of Technology (Department of Management
    Studies)
*MSc   Management Studies.

University of Manchester (Manchester Business School)
  *MBA   All courses.
  *Diploma BA   All courses.
  *MBSc   P. Time.

University of Manchester (Institute of Science and Technology (UMIST))
  *MSc   Management Sciences, all courses.
  *MSc   Marketing, all courses.
  *MSc   Organisational Psychology, all courses.

University of Oxford (Templeton College, Centre for Management Studies)
  *MPhil   Management Studies.
  *MLitt   Management Studies.
  *MSc   Industrial Relations.

University of Salford
  *MSc   Marketing and a Foreign Language, Employment Studies.
  Diploma in Employment Studies.

University of Sheffield (Division of Economic Studies)
  *MBA   All courses.
  *MA   Accounting and Financial Management.
  Diploma BA   All courses.

University of Strathclyde (Strathclyde Business School)
  *MBA   All courses.

University of Wales (Institute of Science and Technology (UWIST))
  *MBA   All courses.
  Dip BA   All courses.

University of Warwick
  *MBA   All courses.
  *MSc   Management Science and Operational Research.
  *MA   Industrial Relations.

The BGA List of Schools Overseas

Australia
  Melbourne
  New South Wales

Canada
  McGill
  McMaster
  Western Ontario
  York

France
  INSEAD

South Africa
  Cape Town
  Witwatersrand

Spain
  IESE

Switzerland
  IMEDE
  IMI

USA
  Amos Tuck
  Berkeley
  Carnegie Mellon
  Chicago
  Columbia
  Cornell
  Harvard
  Illinois
  Indiana
  Kansas
  MIT
  Michigan
  New York
  Northwestern
  Pace
  Pittsburgh
  San Francisco
  Santa Clara
  Stanford
  Virginia
  Wharton
  Yale

APPENDIX IV

The BGA Postgraduate Students' Loan Scheme

Financed by National Westminster and Lloyds Banks (UK and Foreign Schools) and Barclays Bank (Foreign Schools only)

The Business Graduates Association's Loan Scheme was instituted in 1969 to enable experienced men and women to return to full-time study at postgraduate level in business administration. It is administered by the BGA on behalf of the banks. A summary of the main features follows. Booklets giving full details can be obtained from the schools or the banks.

1. Students must have obtained admission to one of the courses at a business school in the BGA list. In the case of overseas schools, an undertaking to return to the UK after the course is required.

2. Students should have two years experience in industry, commerce, the Armed Forces or public administration. If they do not have a first degree or equivalent, then they must have had at least five years experience. Exceptions in the light of other professional qualifications will be considered.

3. For UK schools, the loan each year should not exceed £1,500 p.a. plus fees, or two-thirds of previous salary plus fees if this is greater. For overseas schools the maximum loan is normally £4,000; this may be exceeded at the bank's discretion. Interest will be charged half-yearly on the balance of the loan at a rate of 4 per cent per annum during the period of study and for up to one year afterwards. Thereafter, interest will be at the rate of 2 per cent over base rate. Interest charged will be added to the outstanding balance of the loan. The repayment period may be up to eight years. (N.B. The figures in this paragraph vary from bank to bank.)

4. There will be a one-time administration charge of 1 per cent of

the amount borrowed. This will be paid by the bank to the BGA and added to each student's loan.

5. The bank may require an interview, and in any case students will be expected to visit the appropriate branch to sign the necessary documentation and agree repayment rates.

6. Loans to students who fail or leave the course before obtaining a qualification will be transferred to the normal debts section of the bank and will be subject to normal terms and prevailing interest rates.

7. Applications must not be sent to the BGA. For UK schools, they must be made to the Principals who will supply details and forms. For overseas schools, students must apply to Area Managers.